Contents

Introduction

Queen Victoria reigned for 63 years – longer than any other British monarch. Her long rule gave us the name 'Victorian' for this period and its ideas and discoveries. In 1837, when she came to the throne, Britain was leading the world in industry and trade. When she died in 1901, there was much more competition from other European nations and America.

In Britain itself the population rose from 15 to 37 million, as new methods of health and child care became more widely available. Many more children went to school in the later part of the reign, so that by 1901 nearly everyone could read and write.

Though the new inventions were made in the name of 'progress', they brought many problems to people at the time. Machines made farms and factories more efficient, but their use caused people to be laid off work. The only 'social security' was in the hated workhouse, and nobody wanted to go there.

Young people who found work as domestic servants could in some ways think themselves fortunate. Though the work was hard and the hours very long, they were at least fed and clothed. By the end of the century, middle-class girls were becoming more ambitious and some limited choices were available to them. Many looked for work as teachers, secretaries, nurses and telephone operators. A few learnt to drive motor cars. However, they did not have many legal rights. Women were still not able to vote, and when a woman married, any property she had went to her husband. When at last there were women's colleges in Cambridge, Oxford and London, women could study for degrees like men, but it was still a struggle.

The pace of life had speeded up by 1901. Telegraphs and telephones linked continents, and newspapers reported foreign events overnight. Photographs were replacing artists' impressions of important happenings. Travel was simpler and faster. People talked with satisfaction of the 'progress' Britain had made since Victoria's coronation. There were British 'possessions' all round the world, so that it was said Britain had an Empire 'on which the sun never set'.

IN BRITAIN

1837 Victoria becomes Queen
1838 First Chartist petition
1840 Victoria marries Albert
1842 Mines Act
1845 Irish potato famine
1846 Repeal of the Corn Laws
1847 Factory Act passed
1848 Last Chartist petition

1851 The Great Exhibition
To 1859 Scottish Highland
     Clearances
1857 Hallé Orchestra in
     Manchester founded
1859 Darwin's *On the Origin of
     Species* published

1860 First modern eisteddfod
1861 Prince Albert dies
1864 Chimney Sweeps Act forbids
     use of children
1867 Parliamentary Reform Act
     gives more men the vote
1868 First TUC Conference
1869 Girton College, Cambridge,
     founded (first women's
     college)

1872 Voting by secret ballot
1875 Public Health Act
1877 Queen becomes Empress of
     India
1879 Tay Bridge disaster

1881 Disraeli dies
1886 Gladstone tries to get Home
     Rule for Ireland
1887 Queen's Golden Jubilee
1889 Forth Bridge completed
1889 Major London dock strike

1890 Free elementary education
1895 Last tollgate closes
1897 Queen's Diamond Jubilee
1901 Victoria dies

ABROAD	CHANGING OUR LIVES	PEOPLE

1840 Treaty of Waitangi
1840–2 Opium War in China
1842 Hong Kong becomes
    British colony
1843 Maori war – revolt against
    British
1848 'Year of Revolutions' in
    Europe
	1837–1849
	The telegraph
	Postage stamps
	Gummed envelopes
	Passenger liner to US
	Network of railway lines
	Safety pins
	Gaslighting
	Chloroform
		1835–41 Lord Melbourne PM
		1837 Charles Dickens writes
		    Pickwick Papers (his first
		    novel)
		1843 William Wordsworth made
		    Poet Laureate
		1846 Robert Liston uses ether
		1848 Edwin Chadwick's report
		    on sanitation

1853 Transportation to Australia
    ends for minor crimes
1854–6 The Crimean War
1857 The Indian Mutiny
1858 British government takes
    control of India
	1850–1859
	Sewing machines
	Lending libraries
	Steel
	Chemical dye (purple)
		1851 Isambard Brunel starts to
		    design Paddington Station
		1854 Florence Nightingale at
		    Scutari in the Crimea
		1855 David Livingstone finds the
		    Victoria Falls
		1855–8 Lord Palmerston PM

1862 England cricket team visit
    Australia
1863 Taiping Rebellion in China
    ends
1865 Accident on Matterhorn,
    Switzerland, makes the
    Alps a 'tourist attraction'
1867 Canada becomes a
    Dominion
1869 Suez Canal opens
	1860–1869
	The Red Cross founded
	London underground railway
	Tarmac on some city streets
	Yale locks
	Transatlantic telegraph link
	    with US
		1859–65 Lord Palmerston PM
		1860s Julia Campbell takes
		    photographic portraits
		1863 Charles Kingsley writes
		    The Water Babies
		1865 Lewis Carroll writes *Alice's
		    Adventures in Wonderland*
		1865 Elizabeth Garrett Anderson
		    qualifies as doctor
		1868–74 Gladstone PM

1875 Britain buys Suez shares
1876 First telephone call made
    in US
1879 Battle of Isandhlwana,
    South Africa
	1870–1879
	Christmas cards
	Bank holidays
	Typewriters
	Electric light
		1871 Stanley finds Livingstone
		    in Africa
		1874–80 Disraeli PM
		1878 Gilbert and Sullivan
		    produce *HMS Pinafore*

1880 First Boer War begins (to
    1881)
1881 Battle of Majuba Hill
1885 The Mahdi takes
    Khartoum, Sudan
1887 Canadian Pacific Railroad
    completed
	1880–1889
	Greenwich Mean Time
	Bicycles allowed on the roads
	Vaccine for cholera
	Fountain pens
		1880–5 Gladstone PM
		1880 William Booth founds
		    Salvation Army
		1882 Conan Doyle writes first
		    Sherlock Holmes story
		1883 Bligh wins 'the Ashes'

1898 Battle of Omdurman,
    Sudan
1899–1902 Second Boer War
1900 Three South African towns
    relieved by British forces
	1890–1901
	Motor cars
	X-rays
	Aspirins
	Injection for tetanus
		1892–4 Gladstone PM
		1894 Rudyard Kipling writes
		    The Jungle Book
		1895 Actor Henry Irving given a
		    knighthood

Victoria's life and reign

Princess Victoria was only 18 when she became Queen. In 1840 she married her German cousin, Albert. They had nine children. When Albert died of typhoid, aged only 42, Victoria was very unhappy. She refused to attend to public duties for many years.

A new reign begins

June 20, 1837, London Soon after 6 o'clock this morning, Princess Victoria was awakened by her mother, the Duchess of Kent. The Lord Chamberlain and the Archbishop of Canterbury had come to tell the 18-year-old girl that she had become Queen of England.

Lord Melbourne

Victoria was crowned on June 28, 1838. Her first Prime Minister was Lord Melbourne. 'He is such an honest, good, kind-hearted man and is my friend,' the Queen wrote in her diary. Melbourne taught her the duties of a Queen.

Marriage and family

The Queen could not choose her own husband. Her family decided that her cousin, the son of her mother's sister and a German duke, would be suitable. Victoria waited anxiously to meet him. When she did, she was delighted.

They were married on February 10, 1840. Albert was 20 years old, serious and conscientious. He loved music, and through him Victoria met all the great musicians of the day. The couple usually spoke German together.

By the end of the year Victoria had her first child. In 17 years she bore nine children. Later, by the children's marriages,

The young Royal family in 1848

Queen Victoria in 1901, when she was 81

The Victorian Years

Margaret Sharman

Evans

hers Limited

Published by Evans Brothers Limited
2A Portman Mansions
Chiltern Street
London W1M 1LE

First published 1993

Typeset by Fleetlines Typesetters, Southend-on-Sea, Essex
Printed in Spain by GRAFO, S.A. – Bilbao

ISBN 0 237 51291   2

Acknowledgements

Maps – Jillian Luff of Bitmap Graphics
Design – Neil Sayer
Managing Editor – Su Swallow
Editor – Catherine Bradley

The publishers would like to thank Ken Hills, the English Tourist
Board, the Welsh Tourist Board and the Muswell Hill Children's
Bookshop for their help in the preparation of this book.

For permission to reproduce copyright material the author and
publishers gratefully acknowledge the following:

Cover photographs – (top row, left to right) Hulton Deutsch
Collection Limited, (bottom row, left to right) Hulton Deutsch
Collection Limited, (middle row, centre and right) Mary Evans
Picture Library.

Page 2/3 – Michael Holford; page 8 – (left) Hulton Deutsch
Collection Limited, (right) Mary Evans Picture Library; page 9 –
Mary Evans Picture Library; page 10 – (left) Hulton Deutsch
Collection Limited, (right) Eric Crichton / Bruce Coleman Limited;
page 11 – Michael Holford; page 12 – (left) Robert Harding Picture
Library, (right) Michael Holford; page 13 – (left) Robert Harding
Picture Library, (right) Robert Harding Picture Library; page 14 –
(left, inset) Mary Evans Picture Library, (right) Mary Evans Picture
Library / Town and Country Planning; page 15 – Hulton Deutsch
Collection Limited; page 16 – (left) Hulton Deutsch Collection
Limited, (right) Hulton Deutsch Collection Limited; page 17 –
Hulton Deutsch Collection Limited; page 18 – Norwich Public
Library; page 19 – (above) Hulton Deutsch Collection Limited;
(below) Hulton Deutsch Collection Limited; page 20 – *Illustrated
London News* Picture Library; page 21 – Mary Evans Picture
Library; page 22 – (left) Robert Harding Picture Library, (right)
The National Museum of Labour History; page 23 – (left) Hulton
Deutsch Collection Limited, (right) Mary Evans Picture Library;
page 24 – (left) Hulton Deutsch Collection Limited, (right) Mary
Evans Picture Library; page 25 – (left) Mary Evans Picture Library,
(right) Hulton Deutsch Collection Limited; page 26 – (left)

Margaret Sharman, (right) The Vintage Magazine Co.; page 27 –
Hulton Deutsch Collection Limited; page 28 – (left) Hulton
Deutsch Collection Limited, (right, inset) The Mansell Collection;
page 29 – Hulton Deutsch Collection Limited; page 30 – (above)
Margaret Sharman, (below) Hulton Deutsch Collection Limited;
page 31 – e t archive; page 32 – Michael Holford; page 33 – (left)
Hulton Deutsch Collection Limited, (centre, inset) Hulton Deutsch
Collection Limited, (right) Hulton Deutsch Collection Limited;
page 34 – Mary Evans Picture Library; page 35 – (left) Michael
Holford, (right) Eric Crichton / Bruce Coleman Limited; page 36 –
(left) Hulton Deutsch Collection Limited, (right) Hulton Deutsch
Collection Limited; page 37 – (left) Mary Evans Picture Library,
(right) Michael Holford; page 38 – (left) Mary Evans Picture
Library, (below) e t archive; page 39 – (left, inset) Hulton Deutsch
Collection Limited, (right) Hälle Flygare / Bruce Coleman Limited;
page 40 – (left) The Mansell Collection, (right) Mary Evans Picture
Library; page 41 – (left) Hulton Deutsch Collection Limited, (right)
Mary Evans Picture Library; page 42 – Hulton Deutsch Collection
Limited; page 43 – (left) Robert Opie Collection, Gloucester, (right)
Illustrated London News Picture Library; page 44 – Michael Holford;
page 45 – (left) Hulton Deutsch Collection Limited, (right) Michael
Holford; page 46 – Michael Holford; page 47 – (left) Walter Joseph /
Bruce Coleman Limited, (right) Robert Harding Picture Library;
page 48 – Mary Evans Picture Library; page 49 – (left) Hulton
Deutsch Collection Limited, (right) Mary Evans Picture Library;
page 50 – e t archive; page 51 – (top) e t archive, (left) The Mansell
Collection; page 52 – (left) Military Archive and Research Services,
Lincs, (right) e t archive; page 53 – National Maritime Museum,
Greenwich; page 54 – Hulton Deutsch Collection Limited; page 55 –
Mary Evans Picture Library; page 56 – Mary Evans Picture Library;
page 57 – (left) Hulton Deutsch Collection Limited, (right) Hulton
Deutsch Collection Limited; page 58 – (left) Hulton Deutsch
Collection Limited, (right) Hulton Deutsch Collection Limited;
page 59 – (left) Mary Evans Picture Library, (right) Michael
Holford; page 60 – (Clockwise from top) Michael Holford Limited,
Hulton Deutsch Collection Limited, The Mansell Collection, Peter
Terry/Bruce Coleman Limited, Michael Holford.

The opening ceremony of the Great Exhibition at Crystal Palace. Countries from all over the world came to show their goods and inventions. The exhibition was a huge success.

Britain was linked to most of the royal families of Europe.

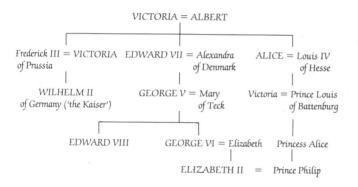

This family tree shows how both the Queen and Prince Philip are descended from Queen Victoria.

The Queen and Prince Albert were a devoted couple. He advised and helped her with affairs of state. They played and sang duets together, sketched and painted. Albert loved his children. He imported Christmas trees for them, following the German custom.

On September 14, 1845, the Queen and Prince Albert moved with their four children to their new home at Osborne, on the Isle of Wight. They preferred it to Windsor Castle, or to Buckingham Palace. They used Balmoral Castle in Scotland as a holiday home. Government ministers had to travel by train and steamship to bring government papers to Osborne House.

The Great Exhibition

Albert was fascinated by scientific discoveries and inventions. He sponsored the 'Great Exhibition', which ran for six months in Hyde Park. Six million people visited it in the newly built Crystal Palace. Many travelled to London for the first time by train, on an excursion organised by an enterprising man named Thomas Cook.

The Queen was delighted with the exhibition. She said the opening day, May 10, 1851, was 'one of the greatest and most glorious in our lives'.

In 1857 the Queen gave Albert the title of 'Prince Consort'. But their happiness ended suddenly. On December 1, 1861, the Prince felt very ill. He got up at 7am to write the draft of an official letter for the Queen. 'I could hardly hold my pen,' he told her. He died of typhoid fever only two weeks later.

The Prince Consort is dead

Dec 15, 1861, Windsor Church bells are tolling all over the country. Prince Albert died last night, in the presence of the Queen. His death from typhoid has shocked everyone. The Queen is bearing her great grief with courage and calmness.

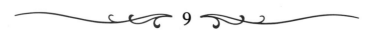

The 'Widow of Windsor'

After Prince Albert died, the Queen was seldom seen in public. She refused to forget him. She surrounded herself with his photographs, visited his grave constantly, had statues erected and buildings named after him. 'My life as a happy one is ended!' she wrote. She wore black, with a widow's cap, for the rest of her long life.

She wrote about their life together at Balmoral, where they had spent many happy hours. Her book, *Leaves from the Journal of Our Life in the Highlands*, published in 1868, was an instant success. Twenty thousand copies were sold in only a few weeks.

Concert hall opened

March 29, 1871, London   The Queen and 8,000 guests attended the opening of the Royal Albert Hall today. The concert hall is near the place where the Great Exhibition was held. A memorial to the Prince is being built nearby.

The Albert Memorial in London

Victoria's Prime Ministers

Altogether there were ten Prime Ministers in Victoria's long reign. Lord Palmerston was Prime Minister when Albert died. While he was in power, Britain sent naval vessels and even armies abroad to show her strength. It was called 'gunboat diplomacy'.

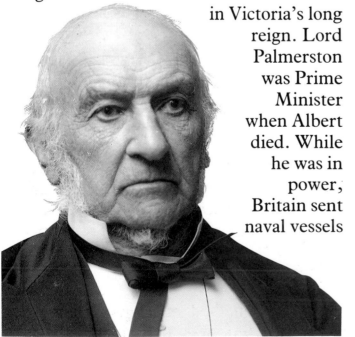

William Gladstone

William Gladstone was Prime Minister four times. He was a great statesman, and a very good speaker in Parliament. The Queen did not like his formal manner. She said he talked to her as if she were a public meeting, not a person.

Benjamin Disraeli, who was Prime Minister from 1874 to 1880, was the Queen's friend. He wore brightly coloured waistcoats and gold chains – quite unlike most Victorian men, in their dark 'morning coats'. He flattered the Queen, and later persuaded her to appear in public again. He was in favour of the Empire (see p. 52), and believed in Britain's 'right' to govern a quarter of the earth. He was also responsible for the Queen's new title of 'Empress'.

What can you find out about the British Empire by looking at this plate?

Queen becomes Empress

Jan 1, 1877, Windsor   The Queen has attended a dinner to celebrate her new title, 'Queen and Empress of India'. She wore jewels from India. The Queen will now sign herself 'Victoria R & I' (*Regina et Imperatrix* – queen and empress).

Victoria's popularity increased when she attended a Golden Jubilee celebration in 1887. Ten years later Britain was in holiday mood for her Diamond Jubilee. A thanksgiving service was held at St. Paul's Cathedral, and people from all over the British Empire took part in a magnificent procession through London.

'A never-to-be-forgotten day . . . The crowds were quite indescribable and their enthusiasm truly marvellous and deeply touching . . . Every face seemed to be filled with real joy.' *Victoria's Diary*, 1897

The Queen died on January 22, 1901, aged 81. Hers was the longest reign in British history.

Families at home

There were great differences between the homes of the rich and poor. Wealthy people had big houses to show their position in society and to accommodate all their servants. Poor families lived in small, unhealthy and often dirty houses.

The grandest Victorian houses had elaborate towers or turrets, ornamental chimneys, and stained glass in some of the windows. Inside, there were many rooms: a drawing room, dining room, library, morning room, study and perhaps a billiard room and a smoking room. On two upstairs floors were the bedrooms, a day and a night nursery and a sitting room for the nanny or governess. Servants' rooms were right at the top. At the back of the house lay the kitchen, pantry, scullery and washroom,

Some Victorian china was very elaborate. This vase was made in Coalport in 1830.

with its copper boiler. There was a lavatory, but not necessarily a bathroom. (You can see some of these rooms on pages 2 and 3 of this book.)

The rooms were full of furniture – mahogany tables and chairs, sofas, and little tables covered with ornaments, photos in silver frames, pottted plants and inlaid boxes. On the mantelpiece you might find stuffed birds, or artificial fruit under a glass dome. There were pictures everywhere.

The master of the house kept to his study and library, or went out to his business or club. The children had to spend most of their time with nanny, in the nursery.

What did the lady of the house do all

A maid clears the table after tea.

day? She called on her friends, wrote letters, and arranged dinner parties, tennis parties, picnics, and rides in the 'ponycart'. Servants did the cooking and cleaning, so there was little for her to do.

There was often a whole array of servants, from the housekeeper down to the little 13-year-old learning to be a scullery maid. The cook and the butler were very important people in the servants' hall. Nobody used their Christian names, and the cook was always 'Mrs', even if she was not married. Supplies were brought to the

There were few machines to help with the housework.
Above: Scrubbing clothes
Right: Boiling a kettle of water

house. The butcher, baker, milkman, grocer and coal-merchant delivered their goods at the back door, which had *Tradesman's Entrance* written on its gate.

Daughters stayed in the schoolroom until they were 18, when they put their hair up and went to balls and parties. Here they met young men looking for wives. A girl could not meet a man without a chaperone – a third person to see that the couple behaved properly.

A young man had to ask a girl's father for permission before he asked her to marry him. If a woman was not married at 30, she was said to be 'on the shelf'. Then she probably became a teacher or a governess. Young men, whether married or single, were drawn to the Church, the Army, the Indian Civil Service or the Colonial Service.

Renting a house
For people such as clerks and shopkeepers, there were houses for rent. Married people rented a full house; single people would rent a room in a lodging house and eat with the family.

Village houses

Victorian paintings of country scenes show romantic thatched or slate-roofed cottages in a perfect sunny landscape. In fact, the cottages were often dirty and overcrowded. Roofs leaked and floor boards were rotten. Water was fetched in a pail from a well or a stream. There was no lavatory. The family collected firewood or bracken for the fire, lit for cooking and for warmth. The chimney probably smoked. Whether the house was built of wood or of stone, the damp crept up the walls. There was usually no guttering, so rain ran off the roof and soaked into the base of the cottage. Windows and doors let in the draught.

Some landlords were concerned about their farm tenants. When Lord Shaftesbury inherited an estate, he rebuilt the cottages, gave his tenants allotments, and built a school for their children.

'Shocking state of cottages; stuffed like figs in a drum. Were not the people as cleanly as they can be, we should have had an epidemic. Must build others, cost what it may.' Lord Shaftesbury, *Diary*, Sept 6, 1851.

By the end of the century, more money was being spent to improve conditions.

Houses in towns

In the industrial towns the population grew rapidly, and more and more houses were built. Some were better than the occupiers' old village homes. Others were crammed together, or built back-to-back, with their front doors opening straight onto the street.

Above: An engraving showing some London slums

Right: The air in most towns and cities was very polluted. This picture shows the smoke from factory chimneys in St Helens, Lancashire.

14

Lunch for the women at the St. Pancras workhouse in London, in about 1900

Thousands of people lived in houses built long before Victoria's reign. Many were in overcrowded, dirty and dark slums, with a single outside tap for several houses, and an earth closet (toilet) for 20 or more families.

> There is nothing picturesque in such misery; it is but one painful and monotonous round of vice, filth and poverty, huddled in dark cellars, ruined garrets, bare and blackened rooms, teeming with disease and death, and without the means . . . of decency or cleanliness. *Illustrated London News*, 1863.

The people who lived in these slums worked in the factories, mills and mines which were making Britain so rich.

Out of doors was no better. Horse manure and domestic rubbish was left to lie too long. (Crossing-sweepers earned tips for clearing a path so that ladies and gentlemen would not soil their shoes or clothes.) Smoke from factory chimneys hung over the roofs and blocked out the sun. In winter, the smoke caused 'pea soup' fogs.

The workhouse

The very poor, old or mentally ill were looked after in the workhouse. Husbands and wives slept in separate dormitories and rarely saw one another. Young children had nothing to do. Unemployed people would rather find work of any kind than go there.

> 'Oliver Twist and his companions suffered the tortures of slow starvation for three months . . . lots were cast who should walk up to the master at supper that evening, and ask for more; and it fell to Oliver Twist . . .
> "Please sir, I want some more." ' Charles Dickens, *Oliver Twist*

Investigations
● Find out if anyone in your family has any Victorian objects in their home. It might be a piece of furniture, for example, or a tile, a piece of china, a postcard or stamp. Can the owner tell you anything about the history of the object?

Farming and industry

More and more people were moving away from the country to towns. There was less work for farm labourers and much more work in the new factories, mills and mines. Thousands of people emigrated to America or other countries, especially from poor farming areas.

Changes in farming

For much of the nineteenth century, farm work was done by hand. Crops were still often planted by throwing handfuls of seed onto the ground from a leather bag – a very old method called 'broadcasting'. Cart-horses were very important, because they pulled the plough and heavy farm wagons.

Some early farm machines were used for threshing grain. From the 1840s there were mechanical reapers. However, many farms still used old methods. Farm workers cut the grain with scythes, and women and older children tied the cut corn into bundles, or 'sheaves'. Country children stayed away from school at busy times of the year, to help with farm work. They scared crows away from the sown seed with huge rattles, herded cattle, and cleared stones away from the fields.

Many farmers could not afford the new machines at first. Most workers disliked them, as more machines meant less work for them. By the end of the century, however, more steam-powered machinery was being used. Thousands of labourers had gone to the new industrial towns to look for work.

Above: A steam ploughing engine in 1874. Straw was used for the fire needed to produce steam. A plough was winched to and fro across a field between two such engines.

Left: The traditional way of haymaking. Hay was cut by hand with scythes.

Famine in Ireland

In Ireland, everyone depended on one crop
potatoes. When the crop failed in 1845
there was a severe famine. Many people
were turned out of their homes because
they had no money for the rent. Thousands
emigrated to northwestern England, or to
America. At the end of Victoria's reign, the
Irish were as poor as ever.

Tragedy as people starve

Dec 25, 1845, Cork Five thousand people are
fighting for scraps of food in rubbish heaps.
They can no longer pay the rent, and have
been turned out of their cottages. They have
already eaten all the cabbage stalks and turnip
tops in the fields. There is nobody to bury
those who die of starvation. Their bodies lie in
the ditches and in the town alleys.

A landlord breaks down an Irish farmworker's cottage
with a battering ram.

In 1846, Sir Robert Peel, the Prime Minister, ended the law that stopped people
importing wheat. For 30 years the 'Corn
Laws' protected farmers from foreign competition. The farmers prospered under
these laws, but bread became too expensive
for the poor to buy. Between 1860 and 1900
the Irish were eating twice as much bread
and far fewer potatoes.

Farming in Wales

The Welsh had a language and culture of
their own. Their landlords were often
English, and this caused ill-feeling. Few
Welshmen had much money to invest in
new projects, and they did not follow new
farming methods. Profits were very low,
and farmers were angry about the tithe
payments which they had to make to the
Church (see p. 45).

Leaving Scotland

In the Scottish Highlands, a great change
was taking place. Landlords wanted land
for sheep. Tenant families were turned out
of their homes, with no work, in what
became known as the Highland Clearances.
A few men earned a little money as shep-
herds. The landlords became rich by selling
mutton to the English.

By the 1850s there were 200,000 homeless people in Scotland. Those who could
pay the passage money emigrated to Australia or Canada.

Island tenants leave

May 30, 1853, Isle of Skye Nearly 300 cottagers
from Skye have left for Australia on the
Georgiana. The agent of the Emigration Department said that 'many of the pigs in
England are better fed and better housed than
are the poor of this island'. The *Georgiana* is
well stocked with food for the journey.

Thousands of tenant farmers left Scotland. When the army looked for volunteers
for Highland regiments to fight in the
Crimean War, they found an empty land.

'We have no country to fight for. You
robbed us of our country and gave it to
the sheep. Therefore, since you have
preferred sheep to men, let sheep defend you!' A newspaper report, 1854.

The fishing industry

Before the railways reached all parts of Britain, fish had to be dried or salted to keep it fresh until it was sold. Now, trains could deliver fresh fish quickly, so salting was not necessary.

Yarmouth, on the Norfolk coast, was the largest herring-fishing port in the world. Fishermen went out in all weathers. When they returned, a team of fishergirls processed the fish. Many of the girls came from Scotland. As the herrings moved south during the summer and autumn, so the girls went from port to port. They could gut and clean up to 1,500 fish each in one hour. Then they sorted the fish into boxes, and loaded them on to ships bound up the Thames to Billingsgate market in London. Women also made and mended the nets – a finger-numbing job in cold weather.

Further south, at Colchester, oyster fishermen sailed their fresh catches up the Thames to London. Oysters can live for days out of water. They were cheap, and they became the food of the London poor. Today they have become a luxury food.

Steamships

From 1885, Grimsby, Hull and Lowestoft shipyards built steamships which were used for fishing. Coal fires in the ship heated water in a boiler to provide the steam. Its pressure drove huge wheels (paddles) on both sides of the ship. A ship powered by steam no longer relied on wind, although many ships also had sails.

Steamships also took cargoes of coal and iron ore to the factory towns. They brought timber from Sweden and Norway to Yarmouth, for ship-building.

Sailing down the east coast was dangerous. Every week the newspapers carried reports of shipwrecks. The sea charts were very unreliable, and dangerous sandbanks shifted with the tide. Most ports had lifeboats, and a crew of brave lifeboatmen, who wore life jackets made of cork.

In 1837 the paddle-steamer *Great Western* was launched. She was the first steamer to cross the Atlantic on regular voyages. A larger ship, the *Great Eastern*, was launched in 1858. Their designer, Isambard Kingdom Brunel, was a brilliant engineer (see p. 47).

Fishergirls at work in Yarmouth harbour

Above: The grand salon of the *Great Eastern*

Right: Isambard Kingdom Brunel in front of the anchor chain of the *Great Eastern*

The *Great Britain*, another ship designed by Brunel, sailed to America on her maiden voyage in 1845. She was the first large iron ship, and was driven by a screw propeller, not paddles.

Long-distance trade

Steam ships crossed and recrossed the seas with trade goods: silks, spices and tea from the East, sugar from the West Indies, raw cotton from America. The ships left British ports loaded with manufactured goods – clothing and shoes, tools, iron goods, cutlery, china and glass. These ships were the largest and most up-to-date in the world.

Fast sailing ships called clippers brought tea from China. Each clipper captain tried to get home first, in order to sell the freshest cargo of tea.

Taeping wins clipper race

Sept 6, 1866, East India Dock, London In May sixteen clippers left China for the long run home. They passed pirate-infested islands, and encountered monsoon storms. Three ships, *Taeping*, *Ariel* and *Fiery Cross* were neck-and-neck when they reached the Equator. They piled on the sails to catch every breath of wind. *Ariel* led at the Scillies yesterday, but *Taeping* managed to get through the London lock gates first. She won by 20 minutes. Her crew will share a bonus of £500 for their victory.

Sail beats steam

July 26, 1889, Sydney, Australia Passengers on board the steamer *Britannia* cheered and waved to a gallant sailing ship today as they came into Sydney harbour. Two days ago they overtook the clipper *Cutty Sark*, showing that steam is better than sail on a calm day. Then yesterday the wind got up and *Cutty Sark*, in full sail, streaked past the *Britannia*. She arrived in Sydney harbour a full hour before the steamship did.

The Industrial Revolution

The Industrial Revolution was about 100 years old when Victoria came to the throne. Coal, iron and textiles had become the chief industries in Britain. Whole families went to work in mines, mills and factories. Workplaces were all privately owned, so conditions varied, but even in the best ones, employees worked like slaves.

Coal mines

Coal was the basis of all Britain's industry, for it was the fuel that powered the steam engines. Every factory used steam engines, which drove huge machines.

Until 1870, Britain's miners dug out half the coal used in the world by hand, using picks and shovels. In mining districts everyone was a miner, for there were few alternative jobs. The number of miners more than doubled between 1851 and 1881, as the demand from industry increased. Men hacked the coal out of the seams, and women and children dragged or carried it along the narrow tunnels. Some of the smallest children were 'trappers', who opened and shut gates in the tunnels as the carts went through. The gates were supposed to improve ventilation in the mines, but terrible accidents still happened.

Explosion blasts through mine

Feb 19, 1862, South Wales   A shocking accident occurred today near Merthyr Tydfil. Workers on the surface heard a loud explosion. Smoke and flames shot up the mine shaft. Rescue workers forced water down the shaft but could not save 49 miners and several horses. This is supposed to be a safe mine: workings are divided into sections to prevent flames spreading along the 1½-mile tunnels. At an 'unsafe' mine last month 204 miners died.

The scene of an explosion at the Oaks Colliery, Barnsley in 1866. The miners' cage can be seen hanging loose. This picture was on the front page of the *Illustrated London News* (see p.43).

Moving towards mass production

Iron goods were very popular. From girders for railway stations to door knobs, the Victorians loved iron. Wrought iron was produced as rods, which were heated till they were red-hot, then hammered into shape. Blacksmiths made horseshoes and farm tools from wrought iron.

Cast iron was ideal for making all kinds of objects, from cooking pots to balconies. Hot liquid iron was poured into shaped moulds, which could be used over and over again. This method made it easy to mass-produce goods. Iron, and iron goods were also exported. When steel was invented in 1856, Sheffield began to produce stainless steel table knives and sharp tools.

Raw cotton came from the slave planta-tions of the American South. It was made into cloth in cotton mills in the north of England. Cotton clothes were cheap and hard-wearing. Cloth was at first coloured with vegetable dyes, but in 1856 the first chemical dye, purple, came on the market.

Lancashire was the cotton centre of Britain; Yorkshire and Wales produced woollen goods, and from Scotland came thick rough tweed.

Women working in a Lancashire cotton mill

Coal, iron and textiles were at the heart of the Industrial Revolution. Shipbuilding was important and several ports became wealthy towns.

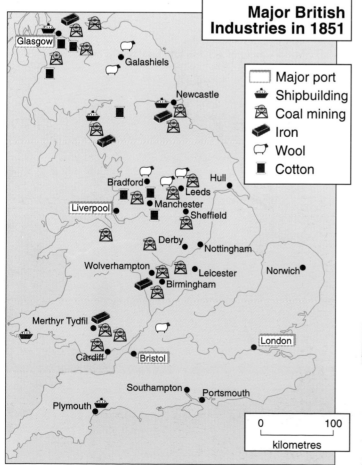

Major British Industries in 1851

Legend:
- ⬜ Major port
- ⛵ Shipbuilding
- ⛏ Coal mining
- ▬ Iron
- 🐑 Wool
- ⬛ Cotton

Glasgow, Galashiels, Newcastle, Bradford, Hull, Leeds, Liverpool, Manchester, Sheffield, Derby, Nottingham, Wolverhampton, Leicester, Norwich, Birmingham, Merthyr Tydfil, Cardiff, Bristol, London, Southampton, Portsmouth, Plymouth

0 — 100 kilometres

Conditions in the mills were often dreadful. Until 1847, when the Factory Act was passed, many children from the age of nine worked very long hours in cramped and airless mills. Much of the machinery was unprotected and dangerous.

Young girl crushed to death

Nov 25, 1842, Manchester Eliza Jenkinson, 28, was walking through a narrow path between two machines when her skirt caught in a cogwheel. She was dragged into the machinery and killed. The mill owner, Mrs Crompton, lost her left arm in the machinery when she tried to help Eliza.

There was also much pollution from factories, and workers were continually breathing coal dust, cotton dust or iron dust. Waste products went straight into the rivers and canals and polluted the water.

The Chartist movement

People were working every day except Sunday, with no holidays. Some thought that a reformed Parliament would help them get better working conditions. The People's Charters of 1838 and 1848 demanded important changes in the way that Parliament was organised.

The People's Charter

May 8, 1838, London On behalf of the crafts-men and industrial workers, we demand: (1) voting rights for all adult men; (2) that Members of Parliament need not be men of property; (3) that MPs should be paid; (4) a new Parliament every year; (5) constituencies of equal size; (6) voting by secret ballot.

The men who wrote the People's Charter were known as Chartists. Most Chartists were peaceful men, but a few were more militant. They were active mainly in the northern industrial regions. A demonstration held in London in 1848 was a failure.

Rain ends demonstration

April 10, 1848, London A Chartist demonstration began and ended on Kennington Common today. The government was expecting trouble, and the Queen was advised to leave London. Special constables, troops, game-keepers with double-barrelled guns, and 1,500 Chelsea pensioners were summoned to defend the city. But no shots were fired. It was pouring with rain, and the Chartists went home. Their petition was taken to Parliament in a hansom cab.

That was the last Chartist demonstration. The new trade union movement took up the fight for better wages and conditions which continued through the century.

Trade unions

The first Trades Union Congress was held in Manchester in 1868. It had a quarter of a million members. Apart from working conditions, the TUC wanted free education, more sanitary inspectors, and for working men to be allowed to be magistrates.

Above: The Houses of Parliament building in London. It was built between 1839 and 1852.

Right: The new trade unions made large, decorative banners to carry on marches. This one shows some of the jobs that union members did.

Labourers' champion an MP

May 9, 1885, Fakenham, Norfolk Mr Joseph Arch, once leader of the Agricultural Labourers' Union, has become a Member of Parliament. Norfolk farm workers hope that their years of poverty and discontent are over. Many of them have been turned off common land, where they killed rabbits to help feed their hungry families. Killing rabbits for food is against the Game Laws.

'I did not put on a black coat. I wore my rough tweed jacket and billycock (bowler) hat . . . I would live and die with my brethren.' Joseph Arch's first day in Parliament.

Benjamin Disraeli (p. 10) said that England was divided into 'two nations': the rich and the poor. The trade unions struggled to close the gap between them. When Disraeli became Prime Minister in 1874, he allowed unions the right to go on strike and carry out peaceful picketing. Now many new unions were formed, especially among the better paid – skilled craftsmen such as shipwrights or engineers.

Match-girls demand compensation

July 18, 1888, Bromley Women working at Bryant and May's match factory have been on strike. They have to handle phosphorus while making the matches. It can cause a terrible complaint which may destroy part of the face. They call it 'phossy-jaw'.

The management promises to improve working conditions, and increase wages. In future there will be a Matchmakers' Union.

The strength of the union movement was shown in the London dock strike in 1889. The dockers closed down what was then the greatest port in the world for six weeks, until they won their demand for a basic wage of sixpence an hour.

Gradually the unions managed to reduce the working day to eight hours, with an agreed minimum wage.

Investigations
● Look out for Victorian farm tools and machinery in museums. Make sketches of them.
● Imagine that you and your friends are workers in a mine or factory in Victorian times. How could you improve your working conditions? What would you change first?

Children's lives

Victorian children from rich and poor families had very different lives. For much of the century, poor children did not go to school, but had to work in coal mines or factories. Some studied on Sundays in 'ragged schools'. Wealthy children were looked after by a nanny in a nursery and saw little of their parents. They had some beautiful toys, such as rocking-horses and doll's houses. Boys were often sent away to boarding school, but girls were usually taught at home.

Children at work

In cast-off clothes and boots (if they were lucky), and living in houses where fleas and bugs were common, children of poor parents did not have much childhood. Thousands got no education at all. In the industrial areas, child labour brought a few necessary pennies to starving families.

Slums in Newcastle-upon-Tyne in about 1880

Better conditions for mining children

June 7, 1842, Westminster Parliament is going to make it illegal for women and young children to work underground. For 13 hours a day small children are chained to coal wagons, which they have to drag through narrow tunnels. Their mothers and sisters haul coal up long ladders to the surface.

The 'climbing boys'

When underground work was made illegal for women and children, many families were worse off than before. Desperate fathers took their children to the children's market, where sweeps hired 'climbing boys' to sweep crooked chimneys. Little boys were sent up the chimney, in narrow spaces in total darkness, to scrape off the soot. Sweeps rubbed salt on the children's knees and elbows to harden them.

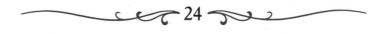

'At first they will come back from their work streaming with blood . . . then they must be rubbed again, and perhaps go off to another chimney.' Sweep giving evidence.

Boys of six were said to be of a 'nice trainable age'. Many sweeps' boys died of burns or from breathing in dangerous gas.

Left: A 'climbing boy' of the 1850s. Many small boys had to become chimney sweeps after Parliament stopped them working in coal mines.

Right: A ragged school in Edinburgh in 1857. These Sunday schools offered poor children their only chance to learn how to read and write.

Sweep transported

Aug 14, 1847, Manchester The court heard how Tom Price, aged seven, died of suffocation. His master, John Gordon, sent him into a hot chimney at a chemical works. Tom screamed that he was choking, but Mr Gordon would not listen. He has been sentenced to transportation to Australia for 10 years.

April 23, 1863 I have great trouble to get in the school pence – many boys sent home for their money.
June 24, 1863 Very few in school – Wild Beast's show in town.
Dec 15, 1864 Baileys sent home – smallpox.
Teacher's logbook, Southampton.

Sunday school to open

Feb 26, 1845, Windsor A new ragged school is going to be opened by a former chimney sweep. These Sunday schools, Mr Charles Dickens says, are for those 'who are too ragged, wretched, filthy, and forlorn, to enter any other place'.

Children at school

The children who went to school paid a few pence a week to learn the 'three Rs' (reading, 'riting, 'rithmetic), and the Christian religion. Then a Portsmouth cobbler started to teach children on Sundays, free of charge. Soon other people began to open 'ragged schools'.

Gradually education improved as Britain became more prosperous. In many families, children who went to school in the 1860s were the first generation able to read.

In 1870 primary education was made compulsory. School lessons became more interesting, and many more subjects were taught. Both girls and boys could, if they wished, go on to a secondary school. Many had to leave school at 14, however, to earn money. There were training colleges for teachers. More than half of these teachers were women. Newspapers became popular as more people learned to read. The first public lending library opened in Manchester in 1852.

Rich children at home

Children of well-off parents were much more fortunate. They grew up in a nursery, with a nanny, and they could probably read by the age of five. They learnt to play the piano, to draw and paint, and to count. They played with toys such as dolls' houses (see p. 2 and 3), a Noah's Ark with wooden animals, and wooden or tin soldiers. On Sundays, many children had to put their toys away (see p. 44).

Most children in wealthy families saw their parents only once a day, usually between tea and bedtime.

A holiday at the seaside

Even on the beach, boys and girls had to be properly dressed. Nobody thought of sun-bathing. Instead, children went for donkey rides, or built sandcastles, or fished for shrimps in rock pools.

Pleasure boats left from the new iron piers at regular intervals. Kiosks sold drinks, buns and seaside rock, whilst 'novelty' shops sold picture postcards, and little boxes with shells stuck all over them. There was always a crowd round the Punch and Judy show.

People who wanted to bathe covered themselves from throat to knees in a bath-ing costume. They went into the sea from a bathing machine. A horse pulled the mach-ine into the water. Queen Victoria wrote in her diary, 'I thought it delightful until I put my head under the water.'

Bank holidays began in 1871, and 15 years later some workers were given a week's holiday a year, with pay. They took their children by train for a day at the sea.

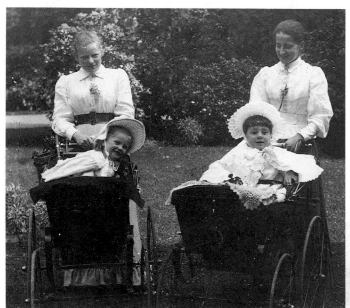

Above: Young children in rich families were looked after by nannies for much of the time. The nanny often took the place of the children's mother.

Right: Seaside holidays became very popular. The bathing machines, pulled by horses, carried people into the sea to bathe.

Sport was very important in public schools. Rugby School invented the game of rugby football.

Education for the rich

Boys from rich families went to public schools, where they learnt Latin and Greek, mathematics, and very little else. By 1860 games had become compulsory. Then it was thought more important and 'manly' to be good at games than at school work. Stories for boys were full of courage and daring, and loyalty to the Empire.

By the end of the century, most public and secondary schools had improved and taught many more subjects.

'Youths come to the Scottish universities ignorant, and are there taught. The majority of those who come to the English universities come still more ignorant, and ignorant they go away.' John Stuart Mill (a writer), 1867.

Oxford and Cambridge Universities taught mainly classics (Latin and Greek), philosophy and mathematics. Many graduates became Anglican clergymen. (Students who did not belong to the Church of England found it hard to get into university.)

By the end of the century, science sub-jects were also taught, partly because of interest in Charles Darwin's work (see p. 33).

Girls were usually taught at home by a governess. A middle-class girl was not supposed to have any ambition. Getting married and having children was 'the best career a girl can have'. She was to be her husband's support, not his equal. This attitude did not change, even at the end of Victoria's reign, when there were good secondary schools available for girls. Even at university (the first women's college opened in Cambridge in 1869), a girl was considered a 'second-class' student.

Ladies can be 'Bachelors'

April 29, 1884, Oxford Women undergraduates will in future be able to take degrees, as men do. Up to now, they took the same examinations as men, but could not become a 'BA'.

Investigations
● Imagine you are a child from a rich Victorian family. Write a postcard to a friend describing your seaside holiday.
● Imagine that you have been sent away to public school for the first time. Write to a friend about your new life.

Travel and communication

There were great changes in transport throughout Victoria's reign. Towns became crowded with horse-drawn buses and hansom cabs. The 'penny farthing' bicycle offered a cheap form of travel. Railway lines sprang up all over the country, and the first cars appeared in the 1890s. Sending letters became much cheaper after the 'penny post' was introduced. Telegraph wires made communication even faster.

Most people travelled from one town to another by coach until the end of the reign. Coaches were expensive unless you travelled on top, in the wind and rain. Any vehicle travelling on main roads had to pay tolls (fees) at special tollgates, and this money paid for the road's upkeep.

Traffic in towns

In towns, you could hire a hansom cab (a horse-drawn carriage), or you could catch the horse-drawn bus, with an open upper deck. Horse-drawn vehicles were common all through the reign.

The penny farthing bicycle came on the market in 1887. Bicycles gave young people freedom to travel. Cycling was much more comfortable once Mr Dunlop's pneumatic tyres were fitted, from 1895.

At the end of the century you might own a car, known as a 'horseless carriage'. But there was no driving test until the 1930s.

Left: A traffic jam in London in 1899. In wet weather horse droppings made the roads very slippery.

Members of the Putney Cycling Club in 1888. Such cycling clubs became very popular.

Travel by rail

The first public railway, between Stockton and Darlington, opened in 1825. In the 1830s and 40s, land all over the country was levelled for railway lines. Tunnels were bored through hills, and viaducts were built over valleys. People were turned out of their homes without compensation to clear land for the railway lines.

By mid-century drivers could really put on speed – provided that the fireman kept shovelling coal into the boiler fire. (Each engine pulled a 'tender', filled with coal.) Chunks of red-hot charcoal often shot out of the funnels, causing fires beside the tracks.

The railways provided employment for thousands of people. Their pay was higher than that of farm workers. At each station there were about 25 different jobs, including a lampman, a luggage labeller and a telegraph clerk.

A fast journey to Paddington

June 13, 1842, London   The Queen has travelled by train for the first time. She left Slough with Prince Albert this morning, on the Great Western Railway. The Prince was worried by the great speed (50 mph).

'Nothing can be more comfortable than the vehicle in which I was put, a sort of chariot with two places. . . . The first sensation is a slight degree of nervousness . . . but a sense of security soon takes its place, and the speed is delightful. . . . The train was very long, and heads were continually popping out of the several carriages. . . .' – Charles Greville's *Diary*, July 18, 1837.

Shocking train disaster

Dec 28, 1879, Firth of Tay, Scotland   As the Edinburgh to Dundee express thundered across the Tay Bridge last night, the bridge collapsed in a high gale. The train plunged into the river, and all the 70 passengers were drowned. This is the worst rail accident Britain has experienced.

Freight that had been carried by canal-boat, or by sea up and down the coast, or by cart, now went by rail. This was much faster, so towns had fresher food (p. 18).

The world's first underground railway opened in London in 1863. Steam trains ran in tunnels from Paddington to Farringdon Street. Electric trains began to replace the steam trains in the 1890s.

An express train on the Great Western Railway, in about 1890. Most of Britain's railway lines and stations were built in Victoria's reign. Different companies ran railways in different parts of the country.

The 'penny post'

In the early years of Victoria's reign, sending a letter was expensive. You paid for the distance travelled, and for the number of sheets of paper used. To keep the price down, some people filled the page with writing, then turned it round and wrote *across* the page.

There were no envelopes then, so you folded the letter and addressed it on one fold. The person you wrote to (the addressee) paid for it. Thousands of letters were returned because the addressee could not or would not pay the postage. In 1839, the average charge was eight pence. Members of Parliament and other officials paid nothing. They were given a number of 'franks', which they stuck onto their letters.

The first postage stamps came into use in 1840. Their inventor, Rowland Hill, had the simple idea of making the sender pay for a letter before it was posted. A one-penny stamp would pay for a letter to go anywhere in Britain.

More people could afford to use the 'penny post' system and far more letters and cards were sent. Until 1841 the letters travelled by mail coach, which were allowed free through the tollgates. After that they were sent by rail.

Boom in picture postcards

Nov 2, 1900, London The demand for picture postcards continues to be high. Everybody has an album to keep them in. Postmen are kept busy delivering about six million every week. Londoners may receive up to 12 mail deliveries every day.

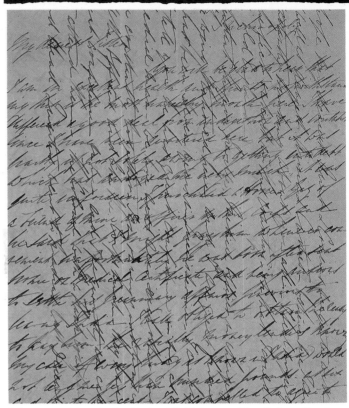

A letter written in India in 1841 by an English sailor to his sister in Norfolk. It begins: 'My dearest Sister, You will be glad to hear that I am in excellent health and spirits . . .'

Cheaper letters on the way

Aug 17, 1839, London Mr. Rowland Hill has invented the postage stamp. The Postmaster General said 'of all the wild schemes he had ever heard of, it was the most extraordinary' – but Parliament thinks it a good idea. The stamps bear a picture of the Queen's head. Mr. Hill believes this design would be difficult to forge. Stamps will be on sale next January, price one penny. The sender will pay for them, not the addressee. They are accompanied by wrappers, or 'envelopes'.

The 'penny black' was the first stamp introduced in Britain.

In the 1870s Christmas cards came into fashion. Many of them were imported from Germany. There they often have snow at Christmas, so artists drew coaches and people in snowy landscapes. This is why we have the idea that in the old days it snowed more in Britain than it does now. It didn't!

The electric telegraph

A month after the Queen came to the throne, the directors of one of the railway companies were shown a remarkable invention: the electric telegraph.

Christmas cards were often very elaborate.

New signalling system introduced

July 31, 1837, Slough Passengers on the Great Western Railway will have noticed the wires, hung on poles, that have recently been put up along the railway line. These 'telegraph' wires carry coded electrical signals. Signalmen can tap out messages on a special machine to warn the next station that a train is on its way, instead of using flags or lamps.

When all British towns were linked by telegraph, the next step was to lay cables overseas. An underwater cable carrying signal wires to Paris was completed in 1851. On July 26, 1866, a cable was finally laid across the Atlantic by Brunel's ship the *Great Eastern* (p.19).

'Railway time'

Until trains and telegraphic signalling came, a person living in Town A did not necessarily keep the same time as a person living in Town B. In fact, most towns kept their own local time. But it is impossible to have a railway timetable based on every town's own idea of the time. So 'railway time' was invented, which might be different from your 'town time'. The whole of Britain kept 'railway time' by 1880, and as 'GMT' we still have it today.

A writing machine

In the 1880s you could buy a typewriter. (Girls who typed in offices were also called 'typewriters'!) The first ones printed the letters underneath the roller, so you couldn't see what you had written until you rolled the paper up. The Queen thought the result was ugly, and her Prime Ministers were told to write to her by hand.

Investigations

● Look out for anything about Victorian railways in your area. You might find old maps or photographs in your local library. Talk to people at your local station and look at the station buildings and bridges. Do you think it was easy or hard to build a railway there?

Inventions and discoveries

Gas and electric light, photography, cinema and the telephone are just some of the inventions of Victoria's reign. People also discovered more about the world around them. Charles Darwin's theories of evolution led scientists to explore heredity in animals. Medical treatment improved considerably after Louis Pasteur proved that germs spread disease. Sterile operations and clean hospitals helped to save many lives.

Gaslight and electric light

Gaslight replaced oil lamps in the houses of the wealthy from the 1840s – though it was only installed in the main downstairs rooms. In the main streets, each evening a lamplighter went round turning on the lamps with a long pole. The gas was made from coal and stored in every town in cylindrical 'gas holders'.

Joseph Swan's electric light bulbs were on sale in the 1880s. The Houses of Parliament and the British Museum were the first public buildings to be lit by electricity. Unfortunately a workman wiring the Queen's drawing room got a mild electric shock, so she stuck to gas. In fact, gas light was so bright that many houses still used it until the 1920s.

Photography

The first cameras, in about 1840, needed very skilled handling, and were rare. You had to sit very still for minutes on end, for the shutter speed was very slow. Every cameraman developed his own photos.

Roger Fenton, who took photos during the Crimean War for the *Illustrated London News*, had a horse-drawn van to hold his equipment: the camera itself, the camera stand, the glass plates on which the negative appeared, and the developing apparatus. It weighed about 40 kilogrammes!

In the 1860s Mrs Julia Campbell began to take pictures of celebrated people. Darwin and many others came to sit for their photographic portraits.

A very early moving picture show took place in London on February 20, 1896. It was in black and white and the figures moved in jerks, but cinema had begun.

A camera of the 1860s. The glass plate slotted into the side of the camera. All the bottles contained chemicals to develop the picture.

The telephone

In 1876 Alexander Graham Bell of the United States invented the telephone. He demonstrated it to the Queen on January 14, 1878. She said it was 'rather faint'.

It took a long time for telephones to be installed in even the most wealthy houses. To make a call, you had to wind a handle to call the operator, who then connected you. The speaking part of the phone was on an upright stand. The listening part was formed by a small tube, attached with a cord to the stand.

All these inventions gave people a lot to think about. They had to get used to electricity, which you could not see, but which produced heat and light. Their voices could also be relayed over long distances.

A more disturbing discovery came from a scientist named Charles Darwin.

Right: Bell's first telephone call in 1876. Below: Telephone exchanges provided new employment, especially for women.

Science disputes the Bible

Nov 24, 1859, London A new book, *On the Origin of Species*, has been published today. The author believes the world was not created in seven days, as the Book of Genesis says. Plants and animals evolved over millions of years, from a single source, he claims.

Darwin's theory of evolution

Darwin went on a 5-year voyage round the world, collecting specimens of plants and animals. He was puzzled by differences in the same species collected from different countries. He could not believe their remote ancestors had all been created separately. He decided that they had once all been alike. They had evolved, or changed, over millions of years, according to their different environments.

By 1871 people accepted that perhaps animals evolved. Darwin then wrote *The Descent of Man*. Human beings, he said, evolved from apes. There was great opposition to this idea that men and women were not God's special creation. But his theories led later scientists to explore heredity.

Above: Darwin's theory that humans had evolved from apes was ridiculed in many cartoons.

Changes in medicine

For the first half of the century, medical knowledge was very limited. Illness was common. No one knew how infection spread, and the poorer parts of most cities had no proper sanitation. There were three huge cholera outbreaks before 1860. Typhoid was also common. Cholera and typhoid are infections caused by drinking dirty water or eating dirty food.

'I have seen a child lie in a downstairs room in a corner, dead of smallpox, and another dying, and the house full of lodgers eating their meals.' Witness quoted by Sir Edwin Chadwick, 1842.

Sanitation to be improved

July 31, 1848, Westminster Sir Edwin Chadwick's report on the health of our towns and villages has appalled all who read it. Now Health Boards will be set up to demand cleaner water and better sanitation. Most houses have no running water, and outside earth closets are often blocked and overflowing. Though the wealthy have indoor lavatories flushed by water, the drainage pipes lead straight to rivers or cesspits.

Sewers being built in New Cross, London, in 1861. It was hoped this would help to prevent diseases such as cholera and typhoid.

Diseases of childhood

Childbirth was dangerous: one newborn child in six died, and so did many mothers. Half the children that survived died of whooping cough or diphtheria. Others grew up with crooked spines or crippled legs due to rickets, caused by a lack of vitamin D. Rickets was common in children of the poor, particulary those who spent most of the day in factories and mines.

Epidemics of typhoid and cholera were common because standards of hygiene were low. The streets were filthy, and in summer flies and rats spread disease. Another big killer was tuberculosis, or 'consumption', as it was called. This was a long slow illness which killed rich and poor alike, but it was highly infectious in overcrowded slums.

As a result of Sir Edwin Chadwick's report, 130 kilometres of underground sewers were built in London. Even then, the Thames was filthy and smelly. The smell was so bad, on May 27, 1886, that Members of Parliament had to leave the Parliament building, which stands near the river.

Epidemic raging

June 25, 1884, London Although vaccination for smallpox has been compulsory since 1841, too many people still die of the disease. In 1871, 23,000 people died. The present epidemic is less serious. Nevertheless, 1,300 cases have been notified.

Prudent housewives kept some strange-sounding mixtures in the medicine cupboard: *sal volatile* (a white powder also called smelling salts) for fainting; *ipecacuanha* for coughs; opium (or laudanum) as a painkiller. Even babies were given opium in 'soothing mixtures' when they cried. Opium is now known to be a dangerous drug. It is made from the opium poppy.

Hospitals and surgery

Nobody wanted to go to the dirty, over-crowded and cold wards of a hospital, where the sheets were often not changed for weeks. Nurses were usually ignorant and untrained; people thought of them as dirty, lazy and often drunken. After her work in the Crimea (p. 51), Florence Nightingale determined to improve nursing in England. She set up a nursing school at St. Thomas's Hospital in London to provide proper training for the profession.

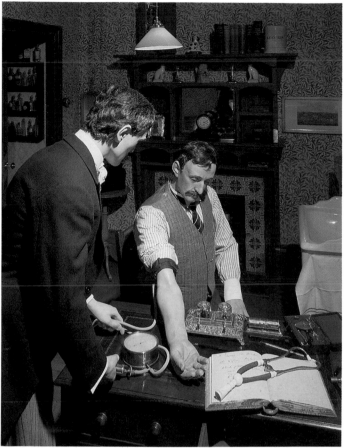

A doctor's consulting room in about 1900. The doctor is measuring a patient's blood pressure. The instruments are similar to those used today.

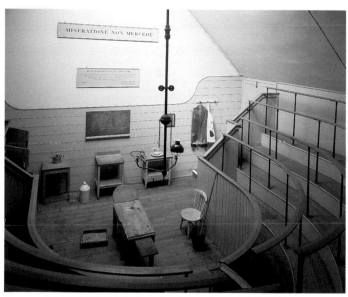

An early 19th-century operating theatre of St Thomas's Hospital in London, which was built in the loft of St Thomas's church. Medical students sat round the edges to watch the surgeon at work.

In the 1840s surgeons thought that if half their patients survived, that was a success. Twenty years later a French scientist, Louis Pasteur, discovered that invisible bacteria or 'germs' cause disease, and proved that people recover better in clean conditions. In England, a surgeon called Joseph Lister used carbolic acid as an antiseptic to kill germs and prevent infections after an operation. This was very successful.

Early in the 19th century, alcohol and opium were the usual anaesthetics for an operation. Better anaesthetics were developed in Victoria's reign.

He didn't feel a thing!

Dec 21, 1846, London Dr Robert Liston has made history by performing the first major operation using an anaesthetic. He placed a pad soaked in ether over the patient's nose and mouth, which caused him to lose consciousness completely until the operation was over.

In 1847 a surgeon in Edinburgh used chloroform for the first time, which caused deeper and quicker unconsciousness. Patients no longer had to endure surgery with only gin to dull the pain.

Investigations

● Find out all you can about Charles Darwin and his sea voyage. Write a letter to a friend as if you were a member of the crew on his ship. Describe some of the strange animals you have seen. Include some drawings if you like.

Entertainment and sport

Victorians, especially the rich, had many forms of entertainment.
Music was very popular, whether at home, in parks or in concerts.
Professional sports also developed, and sportsmen and women became
famous. Major sporting events, like the Derby or the Boat Race,
attracted huge crowds.

Music at home

Ladies who lived in grand houses could usually play the piano and sing. After dinner, friends sat down for 'a little music'. The piano, like other Victorian furniture, was often highly decorated, with brackets for candles at each end. As a guest, you brought music to entertain the others.

Live music was very important before gramophone records were made. The first ones came from America, but they were 'one-off' recordings. To make a second record the singer or player had to perform again! In 1892 a way had been found to take copies of a master record, but not many people knew about this.

Parks and pleasure gardens

Every park had its new bandstand where military bands played marches and popular tunes. Pleasure gardens offered more elaborate entertainments. The Vauxhall Pleasure Gardens in London put on jugglers and conjurers, singers and even pantomimes.

Above: A balloon ascent at Vauxhall Pleasure Gardens in 1849. Huge crowds came to see the fun.

Left: Wealthy Victorians enjoyed musical evenings at home. People took it in turns to play an instrument or to sing.

Music halls

In the 1840s an enterprising gentleman turned his house into an all-male night club. Clients could drink, smoke, sing and watch cheap entertainment. Wives were welcomed in more 'respectable' places, where entertainers told jokes and sang songs. The 'Queen of the halls' was Marie Lloyd. You could buy copies of her songs, the pop hits of the day.

Marie Lloyd in her music hall costume

Theatre

Theatres now put on one play at a performance, with no supporting programme as previously. Henry Irving and Ellen Terry were the most popular actors of the day. Together they played in many great Shakespearean plays.

The Gilbert and Sullivan operas were extremely popular. The comic characters often represented famous people. *HMS Pinafore*, for instance, makes fun of the First Lord of the Admiralty. Audiences loved the song which ends: 'Stick close to your desks and never go to sea, And you all may be rulers of the Queen's navee' – because the First Lord had never been a sailor. He was a bookstore proprietor named W. H. Smith.

A Victorian toy theatre

Concerts and choirs

Many rich people used to attend concerts only to chatter and show off their fine clothes. The Queen and Prince Albert were more serious about music. Audiences began to follow their example.

In 1857, the pianist and conductor Charles Hallé started an orchestra in Manchester. It became one of the best in Britain. The composers Mendelssohn, Liszt, Berlioz and Wagner all performed to packed halls. There were 3,000 people in the audience when Mendelssohn first conducted his oratorio *Elijah* in Birmingham.

In Wales, singing was an everyday occurrence for rich and poor. The industrial towns had choirs of very accomplished musicians, singing in Welsh. Every town and village had its music festival, called an eisteddfod. In 1880 the first National Eisteddfod was held, on August Bank Holiday.

Cricket

Cricket was a very popular game in the nineteenth century, and the greatest batsman of the time was undoubtedly W. G. Grace. During his career he made over 100 centuries, and bowled out batsmen almost 3,000 times. When he was only 18, he scored 224 not out in a match in London.

Until 1864 bowlers delivered the ball 'round arm', not overarm. The bowler's arm was not allowed to swing above the shoulder. Overarm bowling increased the pace of the ball.

England wins back the Ashes

March 31, 1883, London Last year Australia beat England's cricketers for the first time, by seven runs, in a thrilling match at the Oval. The *Sporting Times* said English cricket was dead: 'The body will be cremated and the ashes taken to Australia.' Some lady spectators burnt the bails, and put the ashes into an urn. England's captain, Ivo Bligh, vowed to win this year's match, and recapture 'the Ashes'. And England did win. Ivo Bligh has brought the urn with the Ashes back to England.

The Derby

Horse racing was a favourite sport – 'the sport of Kings' – and Derby Day was a particularly special day. It combined horse racing with the atmosphere of a fair.

'. . . minstrels and beggars and mountebanks [who sold medicines] and spangled persons on stilts and gypsy matrons . . . free-handed youths and young ladies with gilded hair – gentlemen in pairs, mounted on stools, habited in fantastic sporting garments and offering bets to whomsoever listed [liked].' Henry James.

Above: W. G. Grace's Jubilee team, 1898. He is the bearded figure in the centre.

Below: This famous picture of Derby Day was painted in 1856–8.

Mountaineering

Climbing was considered a 'gentleman's sport'. Members of the Alpine Club wore no special clothes and did no training.

By 1865 only the Matterhorn remained unclimbed. When Edward Whymper, aged 25, attempted this dangerous climb with some friends, four people fell to their death. Mr Whymper and the two guides survived. They had alpenstocks (ice axes), and ropes, but these were not very strong. This dramatic accident increased people's interest in the Alps, which became a tourist attraction.

Four killed on Matterhorn

July 14, 1865, Zermatt, Switzerland One man slipped, and the rope attaching the climbers broke on the steep north face. Four men crashed down a 3,000 ft [1000 m] precipice and were killed.

Soccer

Groups of schoolmates or friends started the soccer clubs. Blackburn Rovers were boys from the grammar school, and Sheffield Wednesday were friends who played on their half-day holiday.

Scotland and England disagree

April 4, 1884, London Blackburn beat Queen's Park 2–1 today in a Cup Final that caused an argument. Two Scottish goals were disallowed. The umpire ruled that they were offside. It appears that the Scottish offside rule is different. This will have to be sorted out before they play again.

The Boat Race

The boat race between Oxford and Cambridge Universities on the River Thames was extremely popular. If you could afford it, you hired a steam boat and followed the rowers. Otherwise you joined the huge crowd lining both banks of the river. Rowers wore long trousers and straw hats.

Above: Wealthy climbers in the Alps in the 1860s. Women still had to climb in long skirts.

Right: The Matterhorn in Switzerland

Fashion news

Crinolines and bustles came into fashion in Victoria's reign. Later in the century younger women wore 'bloomers' for cycling, but most clothes were not designed for comfort. Fashions were advertised in the new magazines.

Fashions for women

When a young girl left the schoolroom she was ready for adult dress. This meant wearing several petticoats, tight corsets, and a full skirt.

In the 1850s a new fashion came from Paris – the crinoline. Women tied a metal 'cage' round their waists to support a full skirt. Unfortunately some factory girls tried to copy the fashion in very unsuitable and dangerous surroundings.

'She had been caught several times in the machinery in the same way before. . . . She was . . . not a careful young woman, and wore a very large crinoline, which I think was a great deal the cause of her accident.' Inquest on factory worker, 1864.

Then this fashion had to change so that ladies could climb on to the new double-decker horse-buses. The full skirt was pushed to the back, into a bustle. There were dress factories now, equipped with sewing machines. Mrs Amelia Bloomer shocked many people by wearing full Turkish trousers ('bloomers') for cycling. By the end of the century, clothes had become straighter and more practical, but even sports clothes were difficult to move in.

Left: This fashion plate shows the large bustle of the 1880s.

Far left: The crinoline was popular in the middle of the century. This picture was taken in 1862.

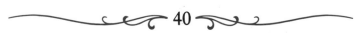

Left: Fashionable gentlemen in 1875. The frock coat, worn by the man on the left, and top hats were typical.

Below: A boy dressed in knickerbockers

Fashions for men

A man of fashion wore a frock-coat and tight trousers in a dark material. He had a large cravat at his throat. His hair was fairly long, and he wore side whiskers – later a full beard. You could tell a man's social standing by his clothes. 'Gentlemen' wore top hats, the middle classes wore bowlers, and workers wore cloth caps. If a clerk or shop assistant dressed himself up as a 'toff' (slang for a rich, well-dressed person), his friends would say he was 'aping [copying] his betters'. It was not thought proper behaviour to do so.

Children's clothes

Wealthy children, both boys and girls, wore sailor suits when they were little. Older girls wore short dresses with full skirts, and over the skirt a pinafore with pockets. Their hair was long, and pulled back from the forehead, to be tied with a ribbon at the back. They wore socks, and ankle-strap shoes indoors, buttoned-up boots out of doors. Coats were also wide-skirted, with a muff to keep their hands warm.

Boys of school age wore shirts, knicker-bockers, long socks, boots, and a cap.

Draper's employee designs dresses

Sept 6, 1857, London   At Swan & Edgar's shop in Piccadilly, Mr Charles Worth makes up dresses of his own design in muslin. His customers try these on, then order the style they like most in materials of their choice. Mr Worth is buying top-quality silks, velvets and brocades from France. He plans soon to open a 'fashion house'.

Fashion and shopping

Charles Worth started the first 'fashion house' in London in 1857. He designed clothes for rich customers. Poorer women tried to look fashionable without spending much. They often made clothes themselves, buying only the material and trimmings. New magazines on sale later in the century were full of advice and fashion hints.

Going shopping

Villages were self-contained communities, where you could buy almost anything. Towns offered a bigger choice, but most shops were small. The first bookstalls opened, and manufacturers advertised their goods in the new newspapers and magazines.

Shops in villages

Villages had general stores, where you could buy almost anything, from tin baths to butter. 'Dry' goods, like flour, or sugar, or biscuits, were sold loose. They were weighed and packaged in the shop.

A Suffolk village in 1844 contained these inhabitants: butcher, corndealer, basket maker, plumber, blacksmith, boot and shoemaker, tailor, chimney sweep, bricklayer, carpenter, and wheelwright. There were two inns, which sold spirits (gin was cheap and popular), and two 'beerhouses',

where the householder brewed and sold his own beer.

Shops in towns

Towns had a variety of shops, but there were few department stores and no supermarkets. Butchers sold game birds, such as pheasants and larks. The dairy sold butter and milk. The tea merchant mixed and weighed small amounts of tea, which he folded into little packets. A gentleman called W.H. Smith opened his first bookstall. Tobacconists sold cigars and cigarettes. Secondhand clothes shops catered for the poor.

Every day carts came into the town with vegetables and other supplies. They took horse manure, swept up from the streets, back to the country to spread on the fields.

Until 1886 shops stayed open until 10 o'clock at night. A shop assistant leaving at 10 pm had to be back next morning at 6 am. On Saturdays some shops stayed open until midnight. Street traders sold medicines, matches, cotton and thread, bootlaces, clothes pegs, flowers and cooking pots. The knife grinder and muffin man called from door to door.

A fruit stall in London at the turn of the century. Much of the exotic fruit, such as bananas, pineapples and dates, came from the countries of the Empire (p.52).

Newspapers and magazines

Newspapers and magazines became ever more popular as more people learnt to read. By mid-century there were 12 national daily newspapers. The front page was all advertisements. Inside, the national and international news was reported in great detail, under tiny headlines. You had to look hard to find what you wanted.

The illustrations for the *Illustrated London News* had to be drawn, then cut into a block of wood (engraved). The printing machines were driven by steam. For the Hamburg story, the artist found an old picture of the town and added flames! News of the fire had been brought to England by boat.

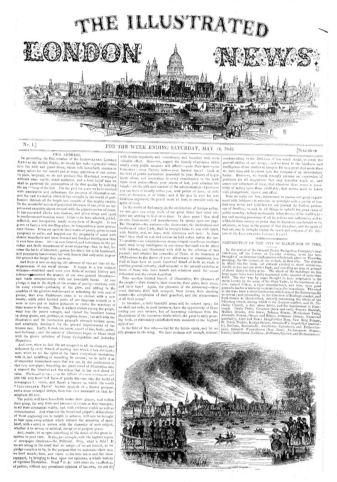

The front page of the first issue of the *Illustrated London News*, 1842

New magazine on sale

May 14, 1842, London The *Illustrated London News* opens its first issue with pictures of a masked ball, held at Buckingham Palace two days ago. Engravers have been working well into the night to finish the 30 illustrations. This 16-page magazine will appear every week, price 6d [then worth about 75p]. It will show really up-to-date news. Another illustration shows a terrific fire in Hamburg, Germany, which occurred only 9 days ago.

An advertisement for Colman's mustard from 1895

Grocer wants your trade

Aug 15, 1870, Glasgow Two pigs, with writing on their sides, were led through the town today. Shoppers stopped to read the message: 'I'm coming to Lipton's, the best shop in town for Irish bacon.'

Investigations
● Design an advertisement for Mr Worth's fashion house (see p. 41). Look at all the clothes in this book to help you.

Church and chapel

We tend to think that most Victorians went to church every Sunday. In fact, less than half the population attended church or chapel regularly. For those who did, mainly the middle class, Sunday was a solemn and important day.

The Victorian Sunday

Most wealthy or middle class families went to a church service in the morning. The rest of the day was spent quietly, reading sermons and prayers and eating cold food prepared the day before. No sporting events were allowed, and theatres were closed. Sundays were particularly dull for children, who were often not allowed to play with their toys.

'I am not at all an admirer or approver of our very dull Sunday, for I think the absence of innocent amusement for the poor people a misfortune and an encouragement of vice.' Queen Victoria

By 'vice', the Queen probably meant that poor people would drink too much gin (only a penny a pint) at the pub.

For most working people, Sunday was their only day's holiday in the week. Many did not attend church, although landlords tried to force them to do so.

Mourning

The Queen did approve of solemn funerals and long periods of mourning. For a year after a death, close relations were supposed to wear black, then, for a further period, purple and grey. Even children wore some form of mourning.

A church in Staffordshire. The decoration was designed by Augustus Pugin, a famous architect who also worked on the Palace of Westminster.

'When the Queen died everyone went into mourning. I had to wear a dark grey suit with a velvet collar. I hated it for replacing my lovely red one with its fur-edged hood. When the mourning period was over, my red suit was too small for me.' Norfolk lady, four years old when the Queen died.

The Nonconformists

Most people in England belonged to the Church of England. People who belonged to other Protestant churches such as the Methodist Church were known as Nonconformists. Wales and northern England had strong communities of Methodists. Many Methodists 'took the pledge' not to drink alcohol. They held services in chapels, which were simpler and less ornamental than churches. There were similar Nonconformist chapels in Scotland.

The Quakers formed another Nonconformist group. They dressed very simply and worshipped in 'meeting houses'. Many Quakers helped the sick and the poor.

In Ireland, few people were Nonconformist. Most were Catholics, and church attendance was higher than in England.

Paying for the Church

Anglican clergymen were paid by the parish. Most of the money came from tithes. In the old days this meant each landowner or tenant had to give up one-tenth of his crops. The amount the vicar got depended on the harvest. In Victorian times the tithes were paid in cash, according to the size of the tithe-payer's land. This meant that even if farmers' profits were low, they still had to pay the same tithe. Riots against this system were very common, but tithes were not abolished until 1936.

Welsh farmers' plight

Jan 31, 1886, Denbigh   Farmers who asked to have their tithes reduced were refused. Most of them hate paying for Anglican clergy as they are Methodists. They are unable to pay because the price of cattle has dropped by two-thirds, so bailiffs are removing their property.

Army to save souls

June 24, 1880, London   Mr William Booth has decided to provide an outdoor 'church', where poor people can enjoy their religion. He will call his band of 'soldiers' the Salvation Army. The Army holds hymn singing and band sessions in the street, often outside public houses.

Above: Many religious groups encouraged people not to drink alcohol. These Victorian plates show the bad results of drinking (left) and the good ones of 'taking the pledge'.

Left: A Salvation Army procession in London's East End, about 1900

Public buildings and monuments

The Victorians liked elaborate public buildings. They built grand town halls and libraries along with new schools, hospitals, railway stations and many churches. Statues and other large monuments were also popular.

Churches and chapels

About 100 new churches and chapels were built in Britain every year. Most of these were Anglican churches, built to serve the new and expanding towns.

Nearly every old church was restored. The money was collected locally, and often the vicar designed new pulpits, screens and altars. The old box pews were taken out and new benches made.

Much of the stained glass in church windows today is Victorian. Some famous painters, such as Sir Edward Burne-Jones, painted the original pictures for them. Church floors were often tiled. Tile-making factories grew up where there was good-quality clay and access to cheap coal for firing. Tiles were also used to line the walls of pubs, hospitals and schools and to decorate fireplaces in new houses.

Schools

The Anglican Church built many schools in the early part of the century. One teacher usually had to teach several groups, all in one room. Later schools were built with classrooms, and boys and girls were taught separately. The schools had gabled roofs, sometimes with a bell mounted on top. After 1870, schools of several storeys were built in urban areas. Most are still in use.

House of glass planned

Oct 12, 1850, London Plans have been published for a building to house next year's Great Exhibition [see p. 9]. It will have no bricks, stones or mortar. In between its cast-iron columns and cross-girders the walls will be made entirely of glass. The architect is Mr Joseph Paxton, who designed the glasshouses at Chatsworth House in Derbyshire.

The building will have 10 double staircases to reach the upper floor, and will cover about 21 acres. Some of Hyde Park's trees will continue to grow inside the building.

The new magazine *Punch*, founded in 1841, was the first to call the glass building 'the Crystal Palace', and the name quickly caught on. Visitors came to the Exhibition from all over the world. Afterwards the Palace was taken down and rebuilt at Sydenham, south London. It burnt down in 1936.

Victorian tiles

Railway stations and bridges

The nineteenth century was 'the railway age' and railway stations are some of the most impressive Victorian buildings. Each railway company in Britain was responsible for its own stations. Great engineers worked on the projects, such as Isambard Brunel who designed Paddington 'after my own fancy'. Main stations had huge wrought-iron girders to support a roof of iron and glass. Such engineering skills, and the materials that made them possible, had not been used before.

New railways needed new bridges, again made from iron. 'Cantilever' bridges, such as the Forth Rail Bridge in Edinburgh, spanned wide river mouths and firths.

Forth Bridge completed

Oct 10, 1889, Queensferry Scottish readers will have watched the two halves of the Forth Bridge being constructed separately, one on either bank of the Firth of Forth. Today the connecting girder was put in place. About 5,000 men have worked on this great project.

Monuments and memorials

Hundreds of the monuments in our towns were built in Victorian times. Some were very tall and elaborate, such as the Albert Memorial in Kensington, London. It was one of the Queen's many memorials to her husband, and was built on the site of the Crystal Palace in Hyde Park (see p. 10).

Statues were a very popular form of memorial to a great general, politician, writer or civic leader. The painter Edwin Landseer designed four huge lions for the base of Nelson's Column in London.

Naval hero honoured

Oct 28, 1843, London The 17-foot [5-metre] statue of Nelson is waiting to be hoisted onto the column built for it in Trafalgar Square. The statue has been carved from Scottish stone and weighs nearly 18 tons. A crowd gathered for a chance to see it yesterday, while it was still on the ground.

The Forth Railway Bridge

The statue of Nelson in Trafalgar Square

Crime and punishment

The towns were full of thieves and pickpockets, many of whom stole because they needed food. Sentences were harsh. A Suffolk girl was transported to Australia for seven years for stealing a watch and a purse.

The conditions in prisons were very bad, with filthy cells and poor food. Prisoners worked from six in the morning until seven at night. Some had to 'pick oakum': they unravelled lengths of old tarred rope which was then used to make boats watertight. Other prisoners broke up stones for road-making. Those fit for 'first-class' work were put on a treadmill, where they worked for hours. Six men walked side by side up the 'everlasting staircase', which was fixed on to a wheel. The wheel turned machinery which ground corn or pumped water.

Other prisoners were transported to penal colonies in Australia (p. 53). Until 1853, people could be transported for having committed minor crimes. They had to build roads and railways in a hot, dry land. Those who survived the harsh regime were set free when their sentences ended. Some found work, and even became prosperous.

Murderers were hanged publicly until 1868, when this was stopped after many protests. An execution was treated as an entertainment. 'Thieves, ruffians and vagabonds crowded to see it', said Charles Dickens.

'My arms, by which I held on to the rail above my head, were quite benumbed, and I could scarcely lift my legs upon the revolving stair . . . I nearly dropped when I fell into my seat at the signal to rest.' *The Windsor Magazine*, c. 1895.

'Brutal jokes, demonstrations of indecent delight when swooning women were dragged out of the crowd by the police, with their dresses disordered, gave a new zest to the general entertainment.' *The Times*, Nov 13, 1849.

Prisoners at work on a treadmill. The dull, repetitive task was also physically exhausting.

A man who could not pay his debts was sent with his family to a debtor's prison, such as the Fleet or Marshalsea. He could not leave, but his family went out every day to earn money, and to bring in food.

Debtors set free

Nov 30, 1842, London The Fleet and the Marshalsea, London's debtors' prisons, are to close. One prisoner in the Fleet, Mr Jeremiah Board, said he had been there for 28 years. He does not know what a policeman looks like, as the force did not exist when he was sent to prison in 1814.

The first police force

The Metropolitan Police Force was set up in London in 1829. Similar forces had developed all over the country by 1860. Policemen were called 'Bobbies' or 'Peelers' after their founder, Sir Robert Peel. They wore blue coats with white buttons

A 'Bobby' of 1856

and a stand-up collar. Their only weapon was a truncheon, and they sounded the alarm with a whistle. The London police headquarters was Scotland Yard. Right at the end of the reign, they started to fingerprint suspects.

The public was fascinated by crime. Sir Arthur Conan Doyle wrote short stories in the *Strand Magazine* about a detective called Sherlock Holmes. They were immediately popular.

An illustration of a Sherlock Holmes story from the *Strand Magazine*, 1893. It shows Sherlock Holmes struggling with his enemy, the evil Moriarty.

'Jack the Ripper'

A real-life crime which alarmed and intrigued everybody became headline news in 1888. The criminal was known as Jack the Ripper, and he murdered prostitutes from London's East End. The Queen followed the case with interest, and even sent the Home Secretary a list of suspects. But 'Jack the Ripper' was never caught.

The army at war

During the nineteenth century, British soldiers and sailors had to fight many times in different parts of the world. At the beginning of Victoria's reign they were sent to China. At the end they were in Africa.

The Opium War

Britain had held a trading base at Canton, in China, for over a century. Traders exported tea to Britain, and imported opium, a drug, from India. Opium was made by drying the juice taken from poppy seed capsules. It was rolled into huge balls and sold by weight.

Everyone in Britain took opium in medicines (see p.34). In China, they smoked it, which was more dangerous as it entered the blood very quickly. Many people died from smoking opium. The Emperor banned it, and opium in British warehouses was burnt.

The British demanded compensation for the loss of their opium. The Chinese refused to pay, so the Foreign Secretary, Lord Palmerston, sent warships and 4,000 troops to China. Much of the Chinese navy was quickly sunk, but the war lasted for two years. In 1842, the Chinese agreed to give Britain the bare and rocky island of Hong Kong as a trading base.

The Taiping Rebellion

In 1851 rebels called the Taipings rose against the Chinese Emperor. They captured hundreds of towns in south China. By the 1860s they had killed 20 *million* people. The British government decided to help the Emperor. In 1863 General Charles Gordon led British and Chinese troops against the rebels, and defeated them.

The Crimean War

In the 1850s the Russians invaded part of the Turkish 'Ottoman Empire'. Britain and

Balls of opium in a warehouse in India

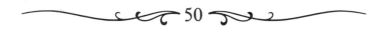

The Crimea Region in 1854

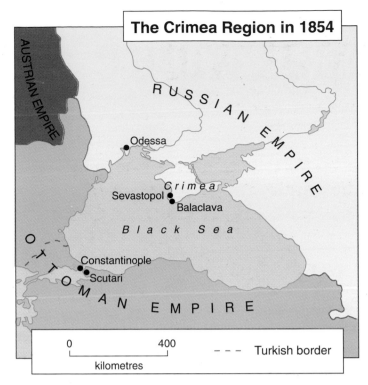

In the Crimean War Britain and France fought Russia, who was attacking the Ottoman Empire. The map shows the most important sites.

France did not want Russia to expand her territory, so they declared war. They landed troops in the Crimea in 1854.

The Crimean War was the first to which newspapers sent 'foreign correspondents'. They provided the first reports and photographs of an army at war. Many of these reports shocked people. The French and British troops spent a terrible winter, in freezing blizzards without proper clothing, equipment or shelter.

Hospital deaths fall

Nov 30, 1854, Scutari Miss Florence Nightingale has taken charge of the hospital. She insists on total cleanliness, and is saving many lives. She never seems to sleep, and wounded soldiers call her 'the lady with the lamp'.

The Charge of the Light Brigade at Balaclava (painted in 1895)

Gallant charge by Light Brigade

Oct 30, 1854, Balaclava Lord Cardigan led 673 horsemen to wipe out Russian guns at the head of a valley. They were fired on by hidden Russian troops from both sides of the valley. Two-thirds of the Light Brigade were killed. There is a rumour that the commander's orders were misunderstood, and the Brigade attacked the wrong guns.

War in Africa

The British and the Egyptians jointly controlled the Sudan, in Africa, and had troops there. In the 1880s a Sudanese holy man known as the Mahdi urged his followers, the Dervishes, to drive out the foreign troops. The British Prime Minister Gladstone (see p. 10) sent General Gordon to the Sudan's capital, Khartoum, to help civilians and soldiers escape. Instead, Gordon decided to defend the town. Gladstone reluctantly sent an army to help him. Before it arrived, the Dervishes had overrun Khartoum, killing Gordon and many of the inhabitants. Many people blamed Gladstone for sending the relief troops too late.

Thirteen years later, the British defeated Sudanese forces at the Battle of Omdurman, near Khartoum. There was great admiration for the courage of the Sudanese.

An expanding empire

At the beginning of the reign, Britain's possessions covered five million square kilometres. By the end of the century, the British Empire, coloured in red on Victorian maps (see page 11), covered nearly 30 million square kilometres – a quarter of the earth!

India

Until 1858, a large part of India was governed by an English trading company, the East India Company. There was an army of mainly Indian soldiers, but all the officers were white. They lived in European-style suburbs, with their families.

Mutineers jailed

May 10, 1857, Meerut, India Indian soldiers have refused to use the new Enfield rifles. Three regiments have mutinied. British officers have been murdered, and the mutineers are marching towards Delhi.

The Indians were angry about the cartridges supplied with the rifles. Before the cartridges could be used, the gunner had to remove a twist of paper, usually with his teeth. A rumour spread that the cartridges were greased with the fat of a pig (which is unclean to Muslims) or of a cow (which is sacred to Hindus). Angry soldiers shot their British officers. The mutiny quickly spread.

In Delhi, the mutineers killed every white person in sight. In Cawnpore, women and children were killed and their bodies thrown down a well. Mutineers who were caught were tied to cannons, which were fired, killing them. After the Indian Mutiny ended in 1858, the British government took control of India.

An Enfield rifle, waterbottle, bayonet and shako (cap)

A cartridge for an Enfield rifle showing the twist of paper

Canada

Up to the 1860s the name 'Canada' applied to a small colony around Quebec. There were other British colonies in North America as well. In 1867 they united, to become the Dominion of Canada. Immigrants flooded into Canada from Britain.

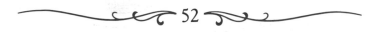

A new Dominion is born

July 1, 1867, Quebec The British colonies have united. Six months ago Mr S. L. Tilley of the colony of New Brunswick hit upon its new name. He heard the 72nd psalm: 'He shall have dominion from sea to sea . . .' 'That's it!' he said. 'We will be the *Dominion* of Canada.'

Twenty years later a 2,700-mile railway, the Canadian Pacific, was completed, and the provinces of the Dominion could at last communicate with one another. The first train took 5,000 soldiers from Quebec to what is now Manitoba to put down rebellions among the native Indians. Many of the Indians had lost their lands to white settlers and were facing starvation.

Australia

Some of the first white settlers in Australia were convicts (see p. 48), sent to 'Botany Bay' (now Sydney). Free immigrants built settlements on other parts of the coast. They imported sheep and managed huge cattle ranches.

In 1851 thousands of hopeful immigrants arrived. Gold had been found at Bathurst, inland from Sydney. It was this gold that made Australia prosperous. The population trebled and trade increased. Roads and railways, schools and hospitals followed. On 1 January, 1901, Australia became a Commonwealth.

New Zealand

New Zealand under British rule

6 Feb, 1840, Waitangi The Maoris have become British subjects. They agreed to the Treaty of Waitangi at a great meeting. One of their chiefs said that peace and trade were good; but that the Europeans should honour the Maori customs and lands.

The colony began well. The British built mission schools and hospitals for the Maoris, and lent them money for farming. But soon settlers arrived who wanted land for sheep. They burnt forests and planted grass. The Maoris banded together and fought for their lands. In the 1860s there were guerilla wars, which the British finally won. By the 1880s the Maoris had accepted British rule. They had lost much of their land. In 1882 the steamship *Dunedin* brought the first frozen lamb to Britain.

The settlement at Port Darwin, Australia, in the 1860s. Life in these colonies was very hard.

South Africa

Both the British and the Afrikaaners (or Boers) wanted to rule South Africa. There was a third powerful force in South Africa – the Zulus of Natal. The Zulus, armed with only spears and cowhide shields, massacred British soldiers at Isandhlwana in 1879. Scarcely 55 out of 1,800 British survived. Three years later, British troops recaptured the Zulu lands.

The Boer War

In December 1880 the Boers declared that the Transvaal was an independent Boer republic, with their leader Paul Kruger as president. The British sent in troops, and prepared for war. But they were not expecting so much opposition. The Boers were much better at guerrilla fighting and marksmanship, and inflicted serious defeats like that at Majuba Hill in 1881.

Boers win battle of Majuba

Feb 27, 1881, Transvaal At dawn British soldiers climbed Majuba Hill to look down on the Boer camp at Laing's Nek below. But the Boers had climbed nearby hillsides, and they shot first. The British had no shelter from the hail of bullets. Many tried to escape down the hill and were killed as they ran. Of the 365 British soldiers on Majuba Hill this morning, 93 have been killed and 133 wounded.

Above: The Transvaal was difficult country to fight in. Here British soldiers are crossing a river with the aid of a life line.

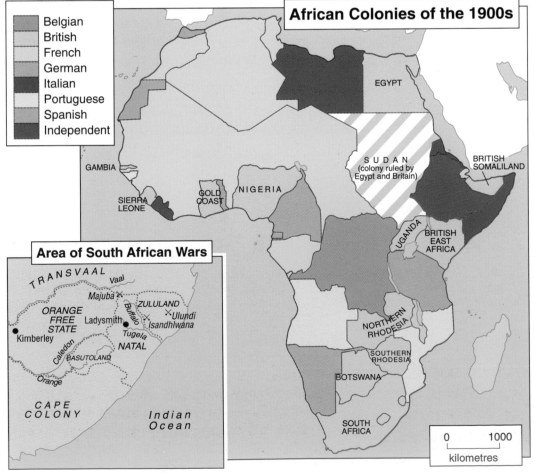

Left: Africa was almost completely governed by European countries at the end of Victoria's reign. Only Ethiopia and Liberia were still independent. Inset: The British, Boers and Zulus fought over the Transvaal region of South Africa for many years. Britain finally won the Boer War in 1902.

After this defeat, the British had to recognise the Transvaal's independence.

Then gold was discovered in the Transvaal. British miners flocked to the mines. When Paul Kruger demanded taxes from them, the British sent in troops again. In 1899 the Boers surrounded three British towns, Kimberley, Mafeking and Ladysmith. The three towns were freed in 1900, but the war went on until 1902.

Egypt

Egypt had its own ruler, the Khedive. His country was heavily in debt, and he invited the British and the French to help him with his finances. It was a Frenchman, Ferdinand de Lesseps, who designed the Suez Canal. It was built by 15,000 labourers, with some jobs advertised for children.

'Labourers under 12 years of age will only receive one piastre, but full rations.'

'See the opening of the great Suez Canal! As steamers may be very fully occupied, early deposits should be made to enable us to secure proper accommodation.' *Cook's brochure*, 1869.

In 1875 Disraeli borrowed £4 million from a banking house and bought Egypt's shares in the Canal for the British government. The British now had great control over the sea route to India.

The scramble for Africa

As late as 1879, most of Africa was unknown to Europeans. By the end of Victoria's reign, the continent had been divided up among the European powers in what is known as the 'scramble for Africa'. At the end of this 'scramble', Britain's colonies included the countries now known as Uganda, Kenya, Botswana, Zambia, Zimbabwe, Malawi, Ghana and Nigeria.

A view of Port Said on the Suez Canal at the turn the century. The canal linked the Mediterranean with the Red Sea. It was a major route for Britain's overseas trade.

The canal became one of the world's most important waterways. It was opened with great ceremony on November 19, 1869. Thomas Cook (p.9) received an invitation, and immediately organised a tour.

Investigations
● Look in newspapers to see what is happening today in countries that used to be part of the British Empire. Would you like to visit any of them?

Famous Victorians

Some brave and adventurous people, such as David Livingstone, went abroad to work as explorers and missionaries. By the end of the century, inventors and engineers had dramatically changed the way in which people lived. Writers such as Charles Dickens helped to make people more aware of the problems of society around them.

The travellers

Whether as explorers, or as missionaries, the Victorians loved to travel. Men and women went alone into lands that had not been mapped, or settled, or even visited, by other white people.

David Livingstone went to South and Central Africa as a medical missionary. He spent years exploring and mapping unknown territory. He learnt local languages and customs, and called slavery 'the open sore of the world'. Livingstone was the first European to see the waterfall that Africans called *Mosi ya Tunya*, 'the smoke that thunders'. He renamed it the Victoria Falls after the Queen.

By 1871 he was ill and exhausted, and he had lost his medicine chest. People wondered what had happened to him. The *New York Herald* sent a journalist, Henry Morton Stanley, to find him. The famous meeting took place on November 10th.

> 'I walked deliberately to him, took off my hat and said, "Doctor Livingstone, I presume".' H. M. Stanley

The missionaries

All over the Empire men and women went to spread Christianity. They taught in mission schools, preached and built hospitals.

Mary Slessor, a poor girl working in a Scottish mill, dreamed of becoming a missionary. The Presbyterian Church agreed to send her to Nigeria, where she worked alone for 20 years. She was a woman of great courage who learnt much about the customs, the religion and the medicines of the tribes with whom she lived.

This cartoon of 1870 shows Dr Livingstone 'unlocking' Africa. Europeans knew little about it before his travels.

Friends of the poor

Many Victorians were concerned about Britain's poor. Some of them built model estates near their factories (such as Bournville near Birmingham and Port Sunlight in Cheshire) where their employees could live.

Octavia Hill helped to house poor people. She borrowed money and bought three derelict cottages, which she repaired. She put in drains, and built water cisterns. Over the years she bought other houses and charged low rents for them.

Octavia Hill

Thomas Barnardo was concerned about the wretchedness of some children's lives. He decided to become a medical missionary, so he went to study at the London Hospital. He was still a student when he opened the first house for homeless boys in Stepney. A few years later he provided a home for girls. Dr Barnardo's Homes still provide shelter and education for children.

The Earl of Shaftesbury and others worked through Parliament to improve working conditions, especially for women and children. He was also a patron of the ragged schools (p.25).

Great scientists

Science was not taught at schools or universities in the early part of the reign. Men like Michael Faraday learnt from other scientists. His great discovery was that a coil of wire can be moved across a magnet to produce an electric current. His ideas led to development of the electric motor, the dynamo, and the telephone.

Michael Faraday

We have seen how Isambard Brunel built bridges, railway stations and steamships using iron (pp.18 and 47). The next stage, how to make steel, was of great importance. An inventor and engineer called Henry Bessemer found out that if you blow air through boiling iron in a 'converter', the iron loses its impurities. The result is steel, which is much stronger than ordinary iron.

A cookery expert

Mrs Isabella Beeton wrote articles about domestic science and cookery in a ladies' magazine published by her husband. They were such a success that she wrote *The Book of Household Management*. Her recipes show the wealthy diet of the time. They used a good deal of meat, fish, eggs, pastry and suet, but not much fruit and few vegetables. Mrs Beeton died, aged only 29, after the birth of her fourth child.

Writers

Charles Dickens, who came from a poor background, first became famous by writing serial stories for magazines. The first one was about a group of characters wandering round England and having fantastic adventures. It was later published as *Pickwick Papers*. Dickens became the most popular author of his day. His novels are a mirror of Victorian life – both the good and the bad. Every book has its comic characters, its heroes and its villains. The novels helped to make wealthy and privileged people more aware of the unpleasant aspects of their society, from bad drainage to transportation.

Charles Dickens

George Eliot was another great Victorian writer. Her real name was Mary Ann Evans, but women often wrote under a male name. She wrote several novels about the changing countryside and towns, and the ways in which people react to one another. Her most famous novels are *The Mill on the Floss* and *Middlemarch*.

The three Brontë sisters, Charlotte, Emily and Anne also used male pen-names. Charlotte, the eldest, wrote several novels. *Jane Eyre*, which partly describes her childhood at an unpleasant school, was a great success. Other novels describe her experience as a governess abroad. Emily Brontë wrote *Wuthering Heights*, a strange love story set in her native Yorkshire. Anne, the youngest sister, also wrote two novels. All the sisters died young.

Charlotte Brontë

Adventure stories have always been popular, and R. L. Stevenson loved telling romantic and exciting tales. He chose the age of Bonnie Prince Charley for *Kidnapped* and *The Black Arrow*. His most famous book, *Treasure Island*, is a tale of lost treasure and exciting encounters with pirates. Stevenson's poor health did not stop him travelling; he died on an island in the Pacific, Samoa, where the inhabitants called him 'Tusitala', the teller of tales.

Right at the end of the century Rudyard Kipling wrote *The Jungle Book*, which Walt Disney made into a cartoon film, and *Stalky and Co.*, one of the first school stories ever written. Kipling was born in India, and he wrote many stories with Indian themes. He also went to South Africa, and wrote army stories based on the Boer War. He was awarded the Nobel Prize for Literature in 1906.

Artists

The Victorians loved pictures which told a story, with titles like: 'A Summer Night', 'Two Strings to her Bow', or 'When did you last see your Father?' They also liked sentimental pictures of children and animals. A favourite artist was Edwin Landseer, who painted the Queen's dogs. Copies of his picture 'Shoeing the Bay Mare' and of an antlered stag against Scottish mountains and sky ('The Monarch of the Glen') were sold in great numbers.

Joseph Turner painted mysterious landscapes and seascapes in oils. His pictures use the effects of light to create atmosphere. Light shines through a storm at sea, and in 'Rain, Steam and Speed' (1844), a train of the new Great Western Railway dashes towards us out of mist and haze. By contrast, the paintings of William Holman Hunt, John Millais and Dante Gabriel Rossetti are a mass of detail. These three were part of the 'Pre-Raphaelite Brother-

A daffodil design by William Morris, and a sample of the original fabric. It cost 6s 11d for a yard [about £7.50 today for a metre].

hood', basing their style on artists who painted before the 15th-century Italian painter Raphael. They portrayed tall, graceful, rather unnaturally beautiful people among trees and flowers.

The Pre-Raphaelites were protesting against the ugliness of early Victorian surroundings. So was William Morris, who hated such things as inkstands made to look like trees, and furniture made of deers' antlers. He designed simple furniture, flowered wallpaper and patterned chintzes.

In the early part of the reign David Roberts toured Egypt and the Middle East, and produced magnificent architectural drawings, with figures in the foreground. Engravings of these appealed to anyone fascinated by these classical places. His very detailed sketches show how these sites have changed in the last 150 years.

Shoeing the Bay Mare by Landseer

For the first time ever

1837 Screw propellor fitted to steam ship
1838 Overseas mail sent to US
1839 Grand National steeplechase at Aintree
1840 'Penny Black' postage stamps on sale
1841 Smallpox vaccination made compulsory
1842 Cadbury's chocolate bars on sale
1843 A few Christmas cards sent to friends
1844 Gummed envelopes on sale at post offices
1846 Operation performed using ether as anaesthetic

1846 Packaged soap powder on sale
1847 Chloroform used for operations
1849 Silver coin, the florin, minted
1850 Half day off granted to workers on Saturdays
1851 First America's cup, won by yacht *America*
1852 A public lending library opens in Manchester
1854 Quinine used to treat malaria
1856 William Perkin discovers Mauveine and Alizarine (purple and red) chemical dyes

1856 Every county has to have a police force
1857 First Victoria Cross awarded
1858 Tower of Big Ben completed

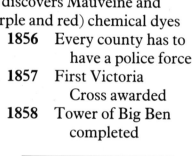

1860 Coins made of bronze come into use
1860 Mt Everest given its present name
1861 A hockey club founded at Blackheath in London
1862 James Glaisher reaches 324,000 feet (c. 9,000 metres) in a hydrogen balloon
1863 Metropolitan Railway, the world's first Underground, opens in London
1865 Penny farthing bicycle invented
1866 Alfred Nobel invents dynamite
1867 New Reform Bill gives more men the vote

1869 Sewing machines used in clothing business
1871 Bank holidays introduced in England and Wales
1871 Rugby Football Union formed
1872 FA Cup: Royal Engineers beat Crystal Palace 1–0
1875 Capt Matthew Webb swims the English Channel
1877 Wimbledon lawn tennis championships begin
1879 London telephone exchange in operation
1880 Education made compulsory up to age 12
1880 National Eisteddfod held in Wales
1882 Some women journalists paid the same as men
1884 Women at Oxford awarded the same university degrees as men
1885 Snooker arrives in Britain (invented by the army in India, 1875)
1886 Largest railway tunnel, the Severn Tunnel, opened
1892 An Indian MP at Westminster, Dadabhai Naoroji
1895 Road speed limit for a car introduced: 12 mph
1895 Season of promenade concerts in London
1896 A wireless station opens on the Isle of Wight
1897 'Big wheel' used at a funfair
1898 Motor vans used to deliver mail
1890 Education becomes free up to age 13

Places to visit and books to read

Many towns in Britain have museums where you can see things made in Victorian times. Some towns or villages have reconstructions of houses or industries. Here are some examples. See if you can find more in your own area. More information is available from the English, Welsh and Scottish tourist boards.

Museums and Buildings

London
Victoria and Albert Museum, South Kensington, London SW7
The Science Museum, South Kensington, London SW7
Bethnal Green Museum of Childhood, London E2
Imperial War Museum, London SE1
London Transport Museum, London WC2
National Maritime Museum, Greenwich, London SE10
(*Cutty Sark* in dry dock in Greenwich)
The Museum of London, London EC2
Dickens House Museum and Library, 48 Doughty Street, London WC1

West and South-West
Museum of English Rural Life, Reading University
Great Western Railway Museum, Swindon
Railway Village Museum, Swindon
Ironbridge Gorge Visitors' Centre, Ironbridge, Shropshire (complex of museums and exhibits including potteries and an ironworks)
Blists Hill Open Air Museum, Coalport, Near Telford, Shropshire (Late Victorian scenes including foundry, shops, chemist, public house, tollhouse, locksmith etc. All working and set over a 50 acre site)
Shambles Museum, Newent, Gloucester (cobbled street with Victorian shops)
Bath Industrial Heritage centre, Bath
Business: a soda wa...
Museum of Costume, E...
Carriage Museums in B...
SS *Great Britain* (histori...
Somerset Rural Life Mu...
Flambards Village Them...
Tintagel Old Post Office, ...
Lanhydrock House, Corn...

Wales
Welsh Folk Museum, St F...
Welsh Industrial and Marit...
sea transport in dockland...
Castell Coch, Cardiff, South ...
Conwy Valley Railway Muse...
Beaumaris Gaol and Court, L...
The Lloyd George Museum a...
Llechwedd Slate Caverns, Bla...
of deep mines and Victoria...
Bobelwyddan Castle, Clwyd (V...
Alice in Wonderland Visitor Ce...
Horse-Drawn Boats and Canal l...
Rhondda Heritage Park, Trehaf...
Cyfartha Castle Museum, Mer...
'Gothic' castle)
Victorian School of the three Rs, ...

South and South-East
Peterborough Museum and Art Ga... ...orough
Hitchin Museum and Art Gallery
Cambridgeshire and County Museum, Cambridge (rural life)
Rural Life Museum, Gressinghall, Norfolk
Strangers' Hall, Norwich (rooms)
Tide Mill, Woodbridge, Suffolk
Cater Museum, Billericay
The Royal Navy Museum, Portsmouth
Tudor House Museum, Southampton
Osborne House, Isle of Wight
Hardy's Wessex Exhibition, Dorchester, (themed ride and tableau)
Staplehill Abbey Crafts Centre, Wimbourne Minster, Dorset

North-West and Midlands
Waterways Museum, Stoke Briserne, Near Towcestor, Northants
Brewery Museum, Stamford, Lincolnshire
Gladstone Pottery, Longton, Staffordshire
Oken's House, Warwick (toys)
Lock Museum, Willenhall
Black Country Museum, Dudley
Rochdale Pioneers Memorial Museum, Rochdale
Southport Railway Centre, Southport, Merseyside
Keswick Museum and Art Gallery, Cumbria
Steamboat Museum, Windermere, Cumbria

North and North-East
Railway Museum, Darlington
Railway Museum, Durham
Open Air Museum, Beamish, Durham (colliery)
Bowes Museum, Barnard Castle, Durham (toys)
National Railway Museum, York
Castle Museum, York (Victorian shops, streets and homes)
Brontë Parsonage, Haworth, North Yorkshire
Industrial Museum, Bradford, West Yorkshire (spinning mill)
Saltaire, near Bradford, West Yorkshire (one of the first estates for workers built by 'reforming' employer
Leeds Industrial Museum, Arnley Mills, Leeds, West Yorkshire
Abbey House Museum, Leeds (Victorian shops)

Scotland
...ltural Museum, Angus, Glamis, Tayside
...Fisheries Museum, Anstruther, Fife
...Castle
...Heritage Centre, Dervaig, Isle of Mull (crofting museum)
...Court Museum, Biggar, Strathclyde
...f Childhood, Edinburgh

...ries of special Victorian interest
..., Millbank, London SW1
...lery, Trafalgar Square, London WC2
...trait Gallery, Trafalgar Square, London WC2
...ery of Scotland, Edinburgh
...Gallery
...ries, Manchester
...rt Gallery
...llery, Liverpool
...Gallery, Port Sunlight
...eum, Oxford
...eum, Cambridge
...Norwich

... all written in or just after Victoria's reign. They will tell
...fe in those days. If you enjoy a particular book look for
...uthor.
...he Water Babies
...s Adventures in Wonderland
...way Children
...t So Stories
...ances Hodgson Burnett *The Secret Garden*
Thomas Hughes *Tom Brown's Schooldays*
Sir Arthur Conan Doyle *The Hound of the Baskervilles*
Charles Dickens *Oliver Twist*

Historical background
These books will tell you more about some of the people of the time, and the things they made and used.
Queen Victoria Lesley Young (*Profiles* series) Evans Brothers Ltd
Florence Nightingale Angela Bull (*Profiles* series) Evans Brothers Ltd
Elizabeth Fry Angela Bull (*Profiles* series) Evans Brothers Ltd
Thomas Edison Josephine Ross (*Profiles* series) Evans Brothers Ltd
Our Victorian Stall (Fundraising for Charity) Beverley Birch (*The Way We Live* series) Evans Brothers Ltd

Glossary

accession: taking up the throne (or any important position)

bailiff: a person sent by the court to collect goods from someone who owes money and cannot pay it

clipper: a fast sailing ship, often used to bring tea from China

colony: settlement in a new country which is governed or ruled by the 'mother' country. The British Empire had colonies all over the world

compensation: an amount of money given to someone to make amends for an injury he or she has suffered

export: something made or grown in one country and sold in a foreign country

guerilla war: fighting by small independent groups

gunboat diplomacy: the use of the threat of force to keep the peace

Industrial Revolution: the rapid development of industry and factories in the late eighteenth and nineteenth centuries

nonconformist: a Christian not belonging to the Church of England or the Catholic Church

picket: someone who stands at the entrance to a company that is on strike, to encourage workers to stay away

sanitation: drainage and disposal of household waste

scullery: small room off the kitchen, used for washing up dishes

secret ballot: voting by putting a marked paper unopened, into a sealed box. In the Chartists' time, voting was not secret. Some candidates saw to it that their workers all voted for them – if they did not they were sacked

Index